Abraham and Sarah

Abraham and Sarah journey through Canaan, accompanied by members of their clan.

Money at its Best: Millionaires of the Bible

Abraham and Sarah
Daniel
David
Esther
Jacob
Job

Joseph
Moses
Noah
Samson
Solomon
Wealth in Biblical Times

Abraham and Sarah

Denise-Renée Barberet

Mason Crest Publishers
Philadelphia

Produced by OTTN Publishing.
Cover design © 2008 TLC Graphics, www.TLCGraphics.com.

Mason Crest Publishers
370 Reed Road, Suite 302
Broomall PA 19008
www.masoncrest.com

Copyright © 2009 by Mason Crest Publishers. All rights reserved.
Printed and bound in the United States of America.

First printing

1 3 5 7 9 8 6 4 2

Library of Congress Cataloging-in-Publication Data

   Barberet, Denise-Renée.
    Abraham and Sarah / Denise-Renée Barberet.
      p. cm. — (Millionaires of the Bible)
    Includes bibliographical references (p.   ) and index.
   ISBN 978-1-4222-0466-5
   ISBN 978-1-4222-0841-0 (pbk.)
   1. Abraham (Biblical patriarch) 2. Sarah (Biblical matriarch) I. Title.
   BS580.A3B36 2008
   222'.110922—dc22
                                       2008011685

Publisher's Note: The Web sites listed in this book were active at the time of publication. The publisher is not responsible for Web sites that have changed their address or discontinued operation since the date of publication. The publisher reviews and updates the Web sites each time the book is reprinted.

Table of Contents

Abraham, Sarah, and Their Wealth	6
Introduction: Wealth and Faith	7
1. Father of Three Faiths	11
2. God Calls Abram	23
3. Abram and Sarai on the Move	36
4. Travels and Travails	50
5. God's Covenant with Abraham	61
6. The Promised Child	72
7. The Ultimate Test	85
8. Patriarch of Many Nations	97
Notable Figures	102
Notes	104
Glossary	107
Further Reading	109
Internet Resources	111
Index	115
Illustration Credits	119
About the Author	120

Abraham, Sarah, and Their Wealth

- The Bible clearly describes Abraham and Sarah as being extremely wealthy. In Genesis 24:35, a trusted servant says of Abraham, "The Lord has blessed my master abundantly, and he has become wealthy. He has given him sheep and cattle, silver and gold, menservants and maidservants, and camels and donkeys." In biblical times, a person's wealth was measured by huge flocks of livestock, extensive land holdings, large families, and unlimited staffs of servants. Most modern millionaires could not afford the affluent lifestyle of the millionaires of the Bible!

- Abraham is not greedy. After rescuing Lot, his family, and the residents of several Canaanite cities from a marauding Mesopotamian army (a story told in Genesis 14), Abraham refuses to accept any reward. Abraham has done what he set out to do; that is reward enough, the text implies. Another story shows how Abraham will not take advantage of others to increase his own wealth. According to this Jewish folktale, Abraham is so respectful of others that his herds are muzzled when they move from place to place, so that they will not nibble at the grass growing in his neighbors' fields!

- Genesis 20:14 describes the expensive gifts that Abimelech, the king of Gerar, gives to Abraham because the king has wronged him: "Then Abimelech brought sheep and cattle and male and female slaves and gave them to Abraham." Abimelech also gives Abraham a thousand shekels of silver and invites him to live anywhere he wishes within his land. The king does these things because he recognizes that Abraham is a wealthy and powerful man who is favored by God.

- Abraham often uses his wealth to help ensure that others prosper. For example, Genesis 13 describes how Abraham and Lot find that their flocks of livestock have become too large for them to continue traveling through Canaan together. Abraham generously offers his younger nephew the opportunity to choose the best pastureland, and agrees to take his herds in the opposite direction.

- Abraham also uses his wealth to spread the revolutionary message that there is only one God. He gives credit to God for his prosperity, and encourages others—whether members of his household, such as family members or servants, or other powerful men, such as the legendary King Nimrod or Abimelech, the king of Gerar—to pray to God and submit to His will for their lives.

Introduction: Wealth and Faith

Many people believe strongly that great personal wealth is incompatible with deep religious belief—that like oil and water, the two cannot be mixed. Christians, in particular, often feel this way, recollecting Jesus Christ's own teachings on wealth. "Do not store up for yourselves treasures on earth, where moth and rust destroy, and where thieves break in and steal," Jesus cautions during the Sermon on the Mount (Matthew 6:19). In Luke 18:25, he declares, "It is easier for a camel to go through the eye of a needle than for a rich man to enter the kingdom of God"—a sentiment repeated elsewhere in the Gospels.

Yet in Judeo-Christian culture there is a long-standing tradition of material wealth as the manifestation of God's blessing. This tradition is amply reflected in the books of the Hebrew Bible (or as Christians know them, the Old Testament). Genesis 13:2 says that the patriarch Abram (Abraham) "had become very wealthy in livestock and in silver and gold"; the Bible makes it clear that this prosperity is a gift from God. Other figures who are believed to have lived during the time period chronicled in Genesis—including Isaac, Jacob, Joseph, Noah, and Job—are described as both wealthy and righteous. The book of Deuteronomy expresses God's promise of prosperity for those who obey his commandments:

> If you fully obey the Lord your God and carefully follow all his commands I give you today, the Lord your God will set you high above all the nations on earth. . . . The Lord will grant you abundant prosperity—in the fruit of your womb, the young of your livestock and the crops of your ground—in the land he swore to your forefathers to give you. (Deuteronomy 28:1, 11)

A key requirement for this prosperity, however, is that God's blessings must be used to help others. Deuteronomy 15:10–11 says, "Give generously . . . and do so without a grudging heart; then because of this the Lord your God will bless you in all your work and in everything you put your hand to." The book of Proverbs—written during the time of Solomon, one of history's wealthiest rulers—similarly presents wealth as a desirable blessing that can be obtained through hard work, wisdom, and following God's laws. Proverbs 14:31 promises, "The faithless will be fully repaid for their ways, and the good man rewarded for his."

Numerous stories and folktales show the generosity of the patriarchs. According to Jewish legend, Job owned an inn at a crossroads, where he allowed travelers to eat and drink at no cost. When they offered to pay, he instead told them about God, explaining that he was simply a steward of the wealth that God had given to him and urging them to worship God, obey God's commands, and receive their own blessings. A story about Abraham says that when he moved his flocks from one field to another, he would muzzle the animals so that they would not graze on a neighbor's property.

After the death of Solomon, however, the kingdom of Israel

was divided and the people fell away from the commandments God had mandated. The later writings of the prophets, who are attempting to correct misbehavior, specifically address unethical acts committed to gain wealth. "You trample on the poor," complained the prophet Amos. "You oppress the righteous and take bribes and you deprive the poor of justice in the courts" (Amos 5:11, 12). The prophet Isaiah insists, "Learn to do right! Seek justice, encourage the oppressed. . . . If you are willing and obedient, you will eat the best from the land; but if you resist and rebel, you will be devoured by the sword" (Isaiah 1:17, 19–20).

Viewed in this light, the teachings of Jesus take on new meaning. Jesus does not condemn wealth; he condemns those who would allow the pursuit of wealth to come ahead of the proper relationship with God: "No one can serve two masters. . . . You cannot serve both God and money" (Matthew 6:24).

Today, nearly everyone living in the Western world could be considered materially wealthier than the people of the Bible, who had no running water or electricity, lived in tents, walked when traveling long distances, and wore clothing handmade from animal skins. But we also live in an age when tabloid newspapers and trashy television programs avidly follow the misadventures of spoiled and selfish millionaire athletes and entertainers. In the mainstream news outlets, it is common to read or hear reports of corporate greed and malfeasance, or of corrupt politicians enriching themselves at the expense of their constituents. Often, the responsibility of the wealthy to those members of the community who are not as successful seems to have been forgotten.

The purpose of the series MONEY AT ITS BEST: MILLIONAIRES OF THE BIBLE is to examine the lives of key figures from biblical history, showing how these people used their wealth or their powerful and privileged positions in order to make a difference in the lives of others.

This Rembrandt painting depicts one of the most famous scenes in religious history: an angel disrupting Abraham before he can sacrifice his son. The Bible says that God asked for this sacrifice as a test of Abraham's faith.

Father of Three Faiths

Approximately 4,000 years ago, in the region that today is known as the Middle East, a man raised his knife and prepared to offer a sacrifice to his god. The man, whose name was Abraham, had no way of knowing that his actions would help to define and shape human civilization.

Although the ancient ritual of sacrifice was common during Abraham's time, there was an important difference. In this case, the creature lying bound on the altar before Abraham was no ordinary bull or sheep, such as might have been sacrificed as a burnt offering to one of the many pagan deities worshiped in the Fertile Crescent. As a young man Abraham had forsaken the polytheistic culture in which he had been raised, deciding to worship and obey a single god. Now, that deity had told Abraham to go into the mountains and sacrifice his beloved son.

It seems impossible that as Abraham raised the knife, he did not feel anxious about what his God had asked him to do. Yet sources that describe the events of Abraham's life indicate that he was fully prepared to submit to the demands of his deity without question—even if that meant killing his own child.

This willingness to obey pleased his god, who sent a messenger to stop Abraham before he could bring the knife to his son's throat. The request for sacrifice had been a test of Abraham's faith, one that he had passed. "Because you have done this and not withheld your son, your only son, I will surely bless you and make your descendants as numerous as the stars in the sky and the sand on the seashore," promised Abraham's god. "Your descendants will take possession of the cities of their enemies, and

Abraham is a major figure in Judaism, Christianity, and Islam. (Left) Illuminated page from a 12th-century French Bible, picturing the initial A decorated with Abraham holding the souls of the righteous in his lap. (Opposite page) An ornate Arab miniature depicting the Angel Gabriel bringing a sheep for Abraham to sacrifice instead of his son.

through your offspring all nations on earth will be blessed, because you have obeyed me" (Genesis 22:16–18).

THE IMPORTANCE OF ABRAHAM

Abraham and his wife, Sarah, are generally considered the first monotheists—people who worshiped only one deity. The idea of a single, all-powerful God who is the creator of the world and the giver of all life was a radically new idea in Abraham's time. Four millennia ago most societies were polytheistic, which means that they acknowledged the existence of many gods. This belief in a universal God, rather than in a large pantheon of gods of varying powers and spheres of influence, was a revolutionary concept that would change the world, ultimately giving birth to three important faiths: Judaism, Christianity, and Islam. As a result, today the spiritual descendants of Abraham make up nearly 60 percent of the world's population.

It is no exaggeration to say that Abraham's importance in biblical history is immense. Abraham's importance can be seen in the fact that he is mentioned some 308 times in the Bible—234 times in the Old Testament and 74 in the New Testament. He is second only to Moses among New Testament mentions of biblical heroes.

Abraham is regarded by Jews and Muslims as their original forefather: the Jewish people trace their lineage to Abraham through Isaac, the son born to him by his wife Sarah, and through Abraham and Sarah's grandson Jacob. Muslims trace their ancestry back to Abraham through Ishmael, the son he fathered with an Egyptian servant named Hagar. For Christians, Abraham's importance lies not in his lineage, but in his example as a man whose faith was so strong that he was willing to do whatever God required. In his Letter to the Romans, the Apostle Paul wrote, "What does the Scripture say? 'Abraham believed God, and it was credited

The Book of Genesis

Abraham's story is told in the book of Genesis, the first book in what Jews call the Hebrew Bible and what Christians call the Old Testament. The stories in Genesis span a period of around 2,350 years. The first 11 chapters of Genesis cover a period of 2,000 years and describe the creation of Earth and human beings, Adam and Eve's fall from grace, Cain's murder of his brother Abel, Noah and the Great Flood, and the construction of the Tower of Babel, an enormous building that was supposed to reach all the way to Heaven. The last 39 chapters of Genesis cover some 350 years and concern Abraham and his descendants, focusing in particular on his son Isaac, his grandson Jacob, and his great-grandson Joseph.

According to a longstanding tradition among Christians and Jews, Moses is the author of Genesis. However, contemporary scholars generally agree that Genesis is the work of four distinct authors or groups of authors who compiled and edited material from different locations and sources over a period of centuries.

During the late 19th century, a theory of biblical authorship called the Documentary Hypothesis was formulated. Over the years there have been numerous variations on this theory. In its simplest form, the Documentary Hypothesis says that the

to him as righteousness.' ... Against all hope, Abraham in hope believed and so became the father of many nations, just as it had been said to him, 'So shall your offspring be'" (Romans 4:3, 18).

WERE ABRAHAM AND SARAH REAL PEOPLE?

The stories about Abraham and Sarah in the Bible and the Qur'an are not the only sources of information about their lives. Because of the importance of Abraham and Sarah, their lives have become the subject of hundreds of legends

---

main blocks of stories in the books of Genesis and Exodus—including most of the story of Abraham and Sarah—are the oldest material. They are attributed to two anonymous authors, known as J and E (the initials come from the names for God that each author uses in the narrative —J for "Yahweh" and E for "Elohim"). Scholars believe these two sets of stories were written down between 950 and 800 B.C.E., although they probably existed in oral form much earlier than that.

Around 600 B.C.E., new material concerned with religious or legal matters—such as the covenant between God and Abraham in Genesis 17, along with genealogical information—was added. This material is believed to have been the work of a priest or group of priests, and is labeled P.

The first five books of the Bible (referred to by Jews as the Torah) were placed in their final form around 400 B.C.E. by a group of editors, who blended the J, E, and P strands together and added new material. The addition is labeled R, after the group of redactors who concentrated on reworking and polishing the text.

Over the past two centuries the Bible has been the subject of intense scholarly scrutiny, and this gives the modern reader a better understanding of how the book of Genesis might have been composed. However, there are still many points of disagreement among scholars, and many of them may be impossible to ever resolve.

and folktales, many of which were written down over the centuries by Jewish rabbis or other religious leaders.

Outside of these religious writings, however, there is no evidence proving that Abraham and Sarah actually existed. Their names are not carved on ancient monuments, like those of kings and rulers. Some secular scholars believe that the entire Genesis account, including the story of Abraham and Sarah, is largely fictional. Just as other cultures have their myths about the creation of the world and the origins of humanity, these scholars argue, Genesis was written to explain the origins of the ancient kingdom of Israel and to glorify its deity, Yahweh. In this context, perhaps the character of Abraham is loosely based on some ancient figure of wealth and influence.

It is extremely unlikely that artifacts dating proving Abraham and Sarah's existence will ever be found. Abraham is believed to have lived around 4,000 years ago. His descendants—both the ancient Israelites (from whom the Jews are descended) and the Ishmaelites (the ancestors of the Arabs)—were nomadic tribal groups who pre-

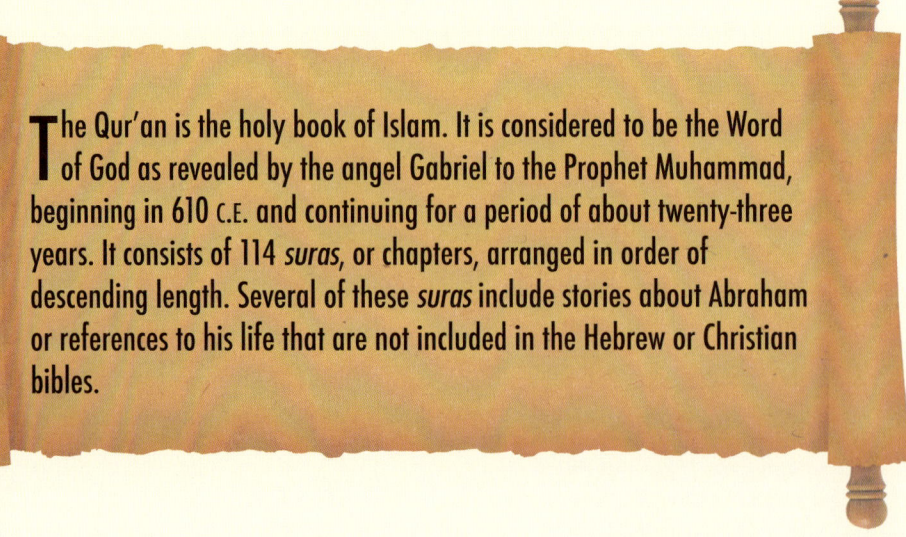

The Qur'an is the holy book of Islam. It is considered to be the Word of God as revealed by the angel Gabriel to the Prophet Muhammad, beginning in 610 C.E. and continuing for a period of about twenty-three years. It consists of 114 *suras*, or chapters, arranged in order of descending length. Several of these *suras* include stories about Abraham or references to his life that are not included in the Hebrew or Christian bibles.

served their stories and traditions orally, rather than in written form. The earliest written Israelite records and stories do not begin to appear until around 900 B.C.E.—about a millennium after Abraham and Sarah are believed to have lived.

Archaeological excavations have given us tremendous knowledge about all aspects of the lives of people from biblical times—from the stories of the great victories and accomplishments of the kings of Egypt and Mesopotamia to the simple, everyday details of what ordinary people

Archaeological excavations provide modern researchers with a great deal of information about life in ancient cities. However, because nomads like Abraham and Sarah were always on the move, no artifacts have yet been found to prove they existed.

MAP OF THE LANDS WHERE ABRAHAM AND SARAH LIVED

ate, drank, and wore. Still, the existence of many of the names of people, cities, and tribes found in Genesis cannot be confirmed by any mention in later written records. Even the time in which Abraham and Sarah would have lived has been hotly debated—and not yet resolved—by scholars. They have been placed anywhere in time from around 2100 B.C.E. to 1500 B.C.E.

The story of Abraham and Sarah—and much of the Old Testament—was long thought to be the compilation and reworking of much older oral traditions that had faithfully preserved the details of their lives. While some scholars continue to believe that the story as told in Genesis is that of actual historical figures, many secular historians now doubt that this can ever be conclusively proven, or that Abraham and Sarah even existed at all.

But even though no one can say for certain whether Abraham and Sarah were real historical figures, or whether all the details of names and places listed in Genesis are correct, the investigations of archaeologists, historians, and other researchers provide a wealth of information about what their world might have been like. Moreover, while the writers of Genesis do not provide elaborate descriptions of people and places, their words are nonetheless so carefully chosen that the modern reader can easily imagine the world that Abraham and Sarah would have seen.

ABRAHAM'S WEALTH

Even accepting that the biblical account is true, Abraham remains an enigma. The Bible tells us nothing about his physical appearance: was he short and squat or tall and lean? Did he have a beard or long hair? Was his voice loud and commanding, or soft and lyrical? Apparently, he is healthy and strong, but even that is a guess, based on information that is not included in the text; never once does the Bible mention that he suffers from any sickness or affliction.

One characteristic of Abraham that *is* clearly stated in the Bible is that he was wealthy. In fact, this particular distinction is made several times. Specifically, Abraham's riches include silver and gold; donkeys, camels, oxen, and sheep; and human slaves—all measures of wealth in the era and culture of his day.

Abraham was the head of a semi-nomadic clan of shepherds and farmers, and on the surface, it does not seem that living the life of a nomad would allow for the accumulation of wealth. However, the late archaeologist William F. Albright speculated that Abraham may have been a caravan leader. Caravans traveled throughout the civilized world, and Abraham may have traded the products his herds produced for whatever he needed along the road.

Canaan, the land promised to Abraham by God, was a favorite trading spot. It lay on the major trade routes between Egypt, Syria, Phoenicia, Babylon, and Assyria. A fertile and fruitful land, it supplied honey, olive oil, grain, wine, and spices to locations throughout the ancient Middle East. Also, the ancient world had a growing need

> There were no coins or paper money in Abraham's day. Instead, people bartered, meaning they traded one thing of value for another. Silver was a common unit of trade, and the value of silver was determined by weight.

This detail from an ornate Jewish prayer book depicts scenes from Abraham's life. (Left) Abraham and Sarah offer hospitality to three angels; (Right) The legendary King Nimrod orders that Abraham be cast into a fiery furnace because of his belief in one God. The page is taken from the so-called Golden Haggadah, a collection of prayers and readings created around 1320 C.E., probably near Barcelona (in modern-day Spain). Jewish families read from a haggadah during the Passover seder; this one is notable for its use of gold leaf in the illustrations, indicating that its original owner was a very wealthy man.

for tar and oil, which Canaan produced in great quantities. So Abraham was surrounded by opportunities to increase his possessions and wealth. But the conclusion we draw from the Bible is that his riches are derived from God. It is God's will, and His alone, which makes it possible for a semi-nomadic shepherd to become the equivalent of what we would consider a millionaire.

And what of Sarah's role? The Bible says that Abraham prospers because of her, albeit for the wrong reasons. Twice, Sarah is taken into the household of kings to be their wife; in both instances, the rulers believe that she is

Abraham's sister rather than his wife. How long Sarah remains with these kings is unknown, and what happened to her during her time with them is also unknown. It is not until Pharaoh and King Abimelech learn Sarah's true identity that she is returned to her husband. And in both instances Abraham is given gifts for her sake. Biblical scholars, in explaining this part of the narrative, point to Sarah's obedience. Her husband, fearing for his life, asks her to lie. She obeys, though this deception puts the Lord's promise to Abraham at risk. In the end, God intervenes, and both Abraham and Sarah are richer for the experience.

Most religious leaders would say that Abraham's importance is as an example of perfect faith in God. Certainly, that is what Paul was thinking in his Letter to the Romans. But it could also be said that Abraham provides an important example of how someone who has been blessed with great wealth should properly behave. Keep in mind that according to the biblical account, Abraham was one of the wealthiest men of his time, owning vast herds of sheep, goats, and cattle, along with gold, silver, and other precious goods. Yet he is not greedy; instead, he often uses his blessings to help others prosper—and to spread the revolutionary message that there is only one God.

Abraham's willingness to challenge conventional wisdom set him apart from all others in his day. This made him open to the call of God, who blesses him beyond measure. As a result, Abraham and Sarah exist in the hearts and minds of billions of people worldwide, and their life stories are incredibly powerful.

God Calls Abram

According to the Bible, Abraham lived until the age of 175. In terms of biblical significance, his life begins at age 75, when God sends him on a long, winding journey across the Middle East. He becomes a friend to God, and God blesses him with untold riches—land, large herds, servants, and sons who produce heirs as numerous as grains of dust on the earth and stars in the sky.

Biblical History of the World

The book of Genesis opens with God's creation of the universe and man, who is made in His image. After creating the first man, Adam, God takes one of Adam's ribs and creates for him a wife, Eve. He provides everything for them, in a place called the Garden of Eden. It is an idyllic, luxurious place, from which rivers flow, and at its center are the tree of life and the tree of the knowledge of good and evil. God tells Adam and Eve not to eat from the fruit of these trees, but they disobey and are subsequently expelled from the garden. Because of Adam and Eve's disobedience, which represents a break in man's relationship with God, human beings then had to toil and labor. Gone was the chance for a life of ease, without pain or suffering, where God the creator takes care of all needs.

Time passes, generations come and go, and humans become more and more disobedient. As a result of their sinful actions, men and women grow more distant from God. Eventually, God sends a great flood to wash the earth clean of all living things. But He spares one man, Noah, as well as his family and animals that Noah takes on an ark he has built, based on instructions from God. But eventually even Noah's descendants slide into sin and disobedience, and begin worshipping idols rather than the one true God.

Rabbinical scholars who have written commentaries about the book of Genesis say that there were 10 generations between Adam and Noah, and then 10

Noah and his family perform a sacrifice to God, giving thanks for their deliverance from the Great Flood. The story of Noah is told in Genesis 5–10.

Genesis 11 tells the story of the Tower of Babel, an attempt to construct a building that would reach heaven. God disrupts this plan; he causes the laborers to speak different languages, so that they can no longer work together. After this, the laborers are scattered all over the world. According to legend, Nimrod, the ruler of Babylon, had ordered the tower to be built; Nimrod would later attempt to have Abraham killed, fearing that he was a threat to his power. This illustration of the Tower of Babel under construction is from a medieval manuscript.

more between Noah and the birth of Abraham, and that throughout this history most humans tried God's patience mightily. But not Abraham. The parable that the rabbis use to describe him is that of a king who has lost a precious pearl. He must sift through great piles of dirt until he can at last find it. Abraham is the pearl, and his exceptional qualities distinguish him from all those who have come before him.

THE STORY OF ABRAHAM BEGINS

Abraham's story begins in chapter 11 of Genesis. The Bible does not say anything about Abraham's early life or how he was led to reject polytheism and worship one God. When readers of Genesis first meet Abraham, he is already 75 years old. He is not yet known as Abraham—that is a name he will receive later—but is instead called Abram.

What the Bible does say is that Abram was born and raised in a city called Ur of the Chaldees. Most people believe this city was located in Mesopotamia (the southern part of present-day Iraq). During the late 19th century and early 20th century, archaeologists excavating an ancient city in this region found artifacts naming the site Ur; in the 1920s, archaeologist Sir Charles Woolley declared that this city, with its enormous ziggurat, was in fact Ur of the Chaldees, because an ancient people called the Chaldeans had once ruled the region.

If this identification is correct, Ur of the Chaldees was a seaport on the Persian Gulf, at the mouth of the Euphrates River, some 12 miles from the traditional site of the Garden of Eden. However, some Islamic and Jewish traditions indicate that Ur of the Chaldees was actually located farther north, in territory that is now part of Turkey.

The great ziggurat at Ur, in modern-day Iraq.

The Fertile Crescent

Mesopotamia is a Greek word meaning "between the rivers"; it refers to the land between the Tigris and Euphrates Rivers, which flow through the southern part of present-day Iraq. Mesopotamia is part of a larger region known to history as the "Fertile Crescent." The region gained this name both for the fertility of its lands as well as for the astonishing creative fertility of the people that this land sustained.

Many important developments in human history took place in the region between the Tigris and Euphrates rivers. Some of the great civilizations and empires that flourished there include Sumer, Babylonia, and Assyria. As Barry J. Beitzel explains in *The Moody Atlas of Bible Lands*:

> In that crescent, mankind developed art, music, literature, mathematics, medicine, astronomy, and chemistry. There the human species learned how to domesticate animals, to cultivate grains and become a food producer, to cluster dwellings and build cities and civilizations, to work metals, and to write (first pictographically and later alphabetically).

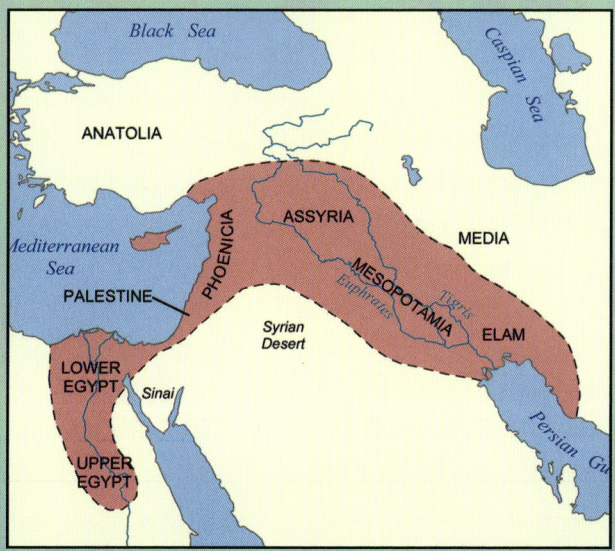

This map shows the region known as the Fertile Crescent.

If the great city of Ur in Mesopotamia was indeed Abram's birthplace, then he would have begun life in a cosmopolitan society. At the height of its splendor, before Abram's time, Ur was a sophisticated city, a center of manufacturing, farming, and shipping in a land of extreme fertility and wealth. It was home to schools and libraries containing thousands of books written on clay tablets. It was also the center of a cult, where the moon-god, Nanna, was king as well as god; the entire city revolved around the cult. Ur was also an important center for trade in the region: donkey caravans carried supplies to and from distant lands, while ships sailed from the docks of Ur down the Persian Gulf with cargoes of copper, quarried stone, and other valuable goods.

In Ur and other ancient cities of Mesopotamia, records were kept on clay tablets, written in a wedge-shaped script called cuneiform.

Although the Bible does not tell us anything about Abram's early years, ancient Jewish lore fills in some of the gaps of his life. Jewish tradition says, for example, that Abram studied in the academy of Melchizedek, a mysterious priest-king who is mentioned later in Genesis. Some scholars believe that Melchizedek taught the secrets of wealth and prosperity, among other lessons, to his students. Other folktales agree that Abram came from a wealthy family, and carried himself in a princely manner. His father, Terah, was an idol merchant.

Flavius Josephus, a Jewish historian who lived in the Roman Empire during the first century C.E., described Abram in this way:

> He was a man of ready intelligence on all matters, persuasive to his hearers, and not mistaken in his inferences. Hence he began to have more lofty conceptions of virtue than the rest of mankind, and determined to reform and change the idea universally current concerning God. He was thus the first boldly to declare that God, the creator of the universe, is one . . . It was, in fact, owing to these opinions that the Chaldeans and other peoples in Mesopotamia rose against him, and he, thinking fit to emigrate, at the will and with the aid of God, settled in the land of Canaan.

THE CHILDHOOD OF ABRAHAM

The Jewish *Midrash*, an extensive collection of centuries' worth of commentary on the Torah by rabbis and Jewish scholars, provides stories, folklore, and legends that elaborate on incidents described in the Torah. There are hundreds of stories about Abram, including a number that describe aspects of his childhood. "When our father Abraham was born, a star rose in the east and swallowed four stars in the four corners of heaven," explains one legend. As a result, the birth comes to the attention of the wizards of King Nimrod. When the wizards learn that a son has been born to Abram's father, Terah, they warn the king that from this child "will issue a people destined to inherit this world and the world-to-come."

Nimrod considers the child a serious threat to his

Who Was Melchizedek?

The Bible describes Melchizedek as "priest of Most High God." Later in Genesis, Melchizedek appears as king of Salem (an ancient name for Jerusalem); after a battle in which Abraham is victorious, Melchizedek blesses him. One of the Dead Sea Scrolls—ancient Jewish writings discovered in a cave during the late 1940s—portrays Melchizedek as a heavenly being who will bring salvation.

Christians view Melchizedek as a prophetic symbol of Jesus Christ. When the priest-king gives Abraham bread and wine in the Genesis account, he prefigures the Last Supper, in which Jesus shares bread and wine with his disciples. Psalm 110:4 says that the messiah will be "a priest forever, in the order of Melchizedek." In his Epistle to the Hebrews, the Apostle Paul claims that the story of Melchizedek is proof that human salvation could not come through the guidance of hereditary priestly groups or strict observance of Jewish law:

> If perfection could have been attained through the Levitical priesthood (for on the basis of it the law was given to the people), why was there still need for another priest to come—one in the order of Melchizedek, not in the order of Aaron? For when there is a change of the priesthood, there must also be a change of the law. . . . And what we have said is even more clear if another priest like Melchizedek appears, one who has become a priest not on the basis of a regulation as to his ancestry but on the basis of the power of an indestructible life. . . . The former regulation is set aside because it was weak and useless (for the law made nothing perfect), and a better hope is introduced, by which we draw near to God. . . . Jesus has become the guarantee of a better covenant (Hebrews 7:11–12, 15, 18, 22).

power, and sends a messenger to Terah asking that he turn over his newborn son. In exchange for the infant, Nimrod offers to fill up his house with gold and silver. Terah replies with a parable: this situation, he says, is like telling a horse, "Let us cut off your head, and we will give you a barnful of barley." Then he lies to Nimrod, saying the child has died, and proceeds to hide the infant for three years in a cave, where with God's help Abram thrives.

When Abram is three years old, he leaves the cave. The *Midrash* explains that it is at this time that he determines there is only one god. According to legend, Abram observes the heavens and prays to the sun, only to see it disappear in the west in the evening. Next, he prays to the moon, but morning comes and the moon, too, disappears, to be replaced once again by the sun. "There is no might in either of these," three-year-old Abram concludes. "There must be a higher Lord over them—to Him will I pray, and before Him will I prostrate myself."

ABRAM AND THE IDOLS

Abram's embrace of monotheism must not have pleased his father, for Terah was a merchant who sold idols—small

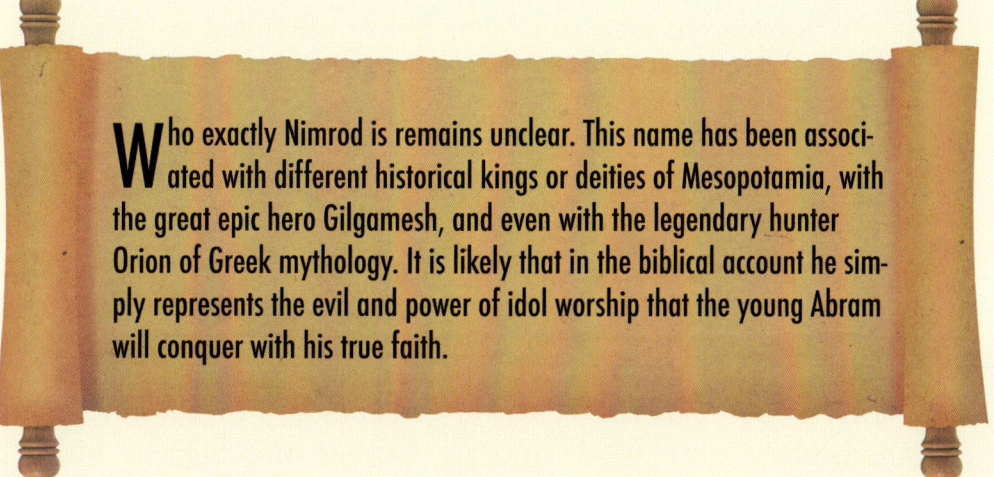

Who exactly Nimrod is remains unclear. This name has been associated with different historical kings or deities of Mesopotamia, with the great epic hero Gilgamesh, and even with the legendary hunter Orion of Greek mythology. It is likely that in the biblical account he simply represents the evil and power of idol worship that the young Abram will conquer with his true faith.

(Above) The sun sets over the Great Ziggurat at Ur of the Chaldees. (Opposite) Four bronze Canaanite idols. Their owners probably believed these idols would help to bring prosperity by ensuring that their fields and livestock were fertile.

clay figures or carved images that were worshiped as gods. People purchased idols in the hope that they would bring the household prosperity.

According to one midrash, Terah entrusts his young son to sell idols at a local market, but Abram mocks the customers, scoffing at what he considers their folly. Another Jewish legend says that one day Abram takes a stick and smashes all of the gods except for the biggest one. Then he places the stick in the hand of this idol and sets him in the center of the mayhem and destruction. When Terah arrives and sees that all his goods have been smashed, he demands to know who has destroyed his idols. Abram explains that the gods began to fight among themselves over food, and he blames the biggest idol among them for destroying the others.

Terah cries out in fury that of course these idols did not do this, because they are incapable of doing anything. Abram responds by telling his father to think about what he has just said. Abram's actions have forced Terah to admit that the idols are nothing but images—powerless pieces of clay and wood.

Terah, however, is so angry at his son's behavior that he turns young Abram over to King Nimrod. Nimrod admonishes Abram, saying that he is lord over all on earth, and that Abram has dared to destroy his gods. But Abram shows that he is not afraid. "If you were Lord of the world, why could you not deliver your own father from death?" he asks the king. "The truth is, as you did not deliver your father from death, so will you not deliver your own self from death."

This insolence makes Nimrod even angrier. "You are playing word games with me," he says. "I bow down to nothing but fire, and I am about to cast you into the midst of it—let the God to

whom you bow down come and save you!" Nimrod's men seize Abram, binding his hands and feet. They pile wood around him and set it ablaze. One version of the story says God saves Abram immediately. Another says that Abram is rescued after standing unharmed in the midst of the flames for three days.

Throughout this ordeal, Abram's brother Haran has been watching. When he sees Abram emerge unharmed from the flames, Haran decides to support his brother's faith. But Nimrod casts Haran into the fire, and he perishes. The rabbinical sources say that the flames consumed Haran because he had decided to believe in God based on the miracle he had witnessed, rather than through faith.

Muslim Traditions Regarding Abraham

With regard to Abraham's childhood, the Qur'an tells a slightly different story than the Bible. For example, in Islamic tradition Abraham is not named Abram when he is born, and his father's name is Azar, not Terah, although he is still described as an idol merchant. When Abraham speaks to Azar in *sura* 19, he is not mocking or contemptuous of his father and his trade. Instead, he expresses deep, loving concern for his father and what might happen to him if he continues to sell idols.

> He said to his father, "O my father, why do you worship what can neither hear, nor see, nor help you in any way?
>
> "O my father, I have received certain knowledge that you did not receive. Follow me, and I will guide you in a straight path.
>
> "O my father, do not worship the devil. The devil has rebelled against the Most Gracious.
>
> "O my father, I fear lest you incur retribution from the Most Gracious, then become an ally of the devil" (Qur'an 19:42–45).

Abraham's father is not moved by his son's words. Instead, Azar warns Abraham that if he rejects the family gods, he will stone him to death. Abraham responds with even more compassion:

> "Peace be upon you. I will implore my Lord to forgive you; He has been Most Kind to me.
> "I will abandon you and the gods you worship beside God. I will worship only my Lord. By imploring my Lord alone, I cannot go wrong." (Qur'an 19:47–48).

THE PROMISED LAND

According to the book of Genesis, when Abram is 75 years old, God tells him to leave Ur and go to an unknown land where he will receive a great reward. Abram sets out for this Promised Land, known as Canaan, "even though he did not know where he was going" (Hebrews 11:8). However, he trusted and followed the Lord's directions.

During his journey to Canaan, Abram would face many challenges and problems; he would also discover that God is the source of all blessings—wealth and prosperity, longevity, security from one's enemies, and even fertility. Although Abram does not always meet God's expectations, he ultimately acquires complete faith in God, and God, in turn, richly rewards him for his faith, obedience, and submission.

Abram and Sarai on the Move

When Abram first leaves his homeland of Ur, he accompanies his father Terah on a journey. Together with his childless wife Sarai; his nephew Lot, the son of his deceased brother, Haran; and their slaves and herds of livestock, they travel about a thousand miles to the northwest. The party probably follows the Great Trunk Road, a major transportation route that ran from Egypt in the south, crossing the Fertile Crescent to cities like Tarsus and Carchemish and Haran in the north.

When Terah, Abram, and their traveling party reach the city of Haran (which is now the village of Harran in present-day Turkey), they stop and settle there. Haran, which means "road," was a great commercial artery. Located about 700 miles northwest of Ur and about 60 miles from the Euphrates River, the city provided travelers with their last vision of green fertile land before entering the vast desert of Arabia. As such, Haran was a strategic location and the site of significant trading activity.

Genesis does not explain why Terah, Abram, and Sarai stopped at Haran. Perhaps someone fell ill on the journey and the party could not go farther. Or, perhaps Terah liked Haran because the people there worshiped the moon god, just like the people in Ur.

One clue to the importance of Haran for Abram's family may lie in Genesis 12:5, which describes Abram's later preparations for the journey to the land of Canaan; the

This ancient carving in Turkey depicts Hittite gods. The Hittites ruled the area north of Canaan, and exerted a strong political and cultural influence over Haran, where Abraham and his father settled.

verse says that Abram took "all the possessions they had gathered and the people they had acquired in Haran." Perhaps the years in Haran—exactly how much time is not known—were spent in trading activity to accumulate goods and wealth that would help Abram settle in a new and unknown land.

Often, "the people they had acquired" is interpreted to mean servants and slaves; these were signs of wealth in the ancient world. Slavery was common in the time of Abram, and the practice is described numerous times in the Torah. However, some rabbinical commentators have another interpretation of this passage, reading it to mean the accumulation of a different kind of wealth: "the people they had acquired" are those whom Abram had converted from idol worship.

Abram Departs for Canaan

Genesis 12 opens with God speaking to Abram. "Leave your country, your people and your father's household and go to the land I will show you," God says. This is quite a demand, so God offers an incredible incentive: "I will make you into a great nation and I will bless you; I will make your name great, and you will be a blessing. . . . [A]ll people on earth will be blessed through you" (Genesis 12:1–3).

Abram is not a young man by any means; on the other hand, we know that he comes from a line of remarkably long-lived ancestors—his great-grandfather and his father both lived to be more than 200 years old. Abram obeys the Lord's call and departs from Haran. But he leaves for Canaan without his father Terah, because the Bible says he died there at the age of 205. (According to Genesis, Terah would have been about 145 years old when Abram left Haran.)

Abram and Sarai on the Move

This illustrated page from a Flemish manuscript of the 15th century shows Abram being called to leave his father's house and travel to Canaan.

Abram's submission to God's will, and his surrender of what makes both him and his family safe, secure, and comfortable, is what makes him such a powerful and

The Nomadic Lifestyle

The word *nomad* comes from the Greek form of a Latin word meaning "to graze." Nomads were wandering shepherds, who moved from place to place with their flocks looking for good pasture and water. They lived simply, pitching their tents in the desert and wilderness areas, and carried all their belongings with them. But nomads also depended on towns and villages, where they could trade for tools and other things they needed.

Nomads are not entirely a thing of the past. Even today, their pitched tents can be found in certain areas of Israel, as well as in other parts of the Middle East and northern Africa. Of course, it's also not unheard of to see modern cars or pickup trucks parked beside a nomad's tent!

This illustration by Gustave Doré, from a 19th-century Bible, shows Abram and his clan driving their livestock to Canaan.

defining figure for Christianity, Judaism, and Islam. As journalist and biblical historian Bruce Feiler explains:

> [T]he Bible says, "I want you to have total trust in me, Abraham." You're not going to know where your next meal is coming from. You're not going to know where your next home is. If you're going to be in covenant with me, you have to trust me with every cell in your body. And if you do that, I will bless you.

God's blessings do not stop with Abram; the last part of God's promise assures Abram that by him—because of and through him—"all the families of the earth" will also be blessed. One rabbinical commentator explains Abraham's journey as the spreading forth of good things throughout the lands:

> [W]hat did Abraham resemble? A vial of scent with a tight-fitting lid put away in a corner so that its fragrance could not go forth. As soon as it was moved from that place [and opened], its fragrance began to go forth. So the Holy One said to Abraham: Abraham, many good deeds are in you. Travel about from place to place, and the greatness of your name will go forth in My world.

HEADED TO CANAAN

God directs Abram to travel to the land known as Canaan. This region corresponds roughly to the present-day states of Israel (including the disputed West Bank and Gaza Strip territories), western Jordan, southern and coastal Syria and Lebanon, and the southern part of modern Turkey. Bounded to the west by the Mediterranean Sea, to the north by mountains, and to the east and south by

Nomadic Bedouin herdsmen guide their sheep along a hillside in the Jordan Valley. In ancient Canaan, nomads like Abraham and his clan could find pastureland and water for their livestock, and trade with settled communities for tools and supplies.

desert, this is a relatively small geographic area—about 10,000 square miles (25,900 sq km), or the approximate size of the state of Vermont. It was not Canaan's size, but rather its location that made it strategically important, both in ancient times and today.

Geologically, Canaan forms a land bridge between the continents of Asia and Africa. Because direct east-west travel was restricted by the extreme difficulty and danger of crossing the Syrian Desert, Canaan provided a natural funnel for travel between established population centers in Egypt and Mesopotamia. This geographical position could be extremely beneficial because of the movement of trade caravans through Canaan. There was ample opportunity for the exchange of skills, ideas, culture, and material wealth. Nomads, merchants, skilled workers, artisans, and even armies would have crossed this land, and their presence would have influenced people such as Abram, Sarai, and members of their clan.

However, Canaan's strategic location also made life there quite precarious. With ambitious empires such as those of Egypt and Mesopotamia close by, the history of Canaan has often been a history of warfare and conflict.

In the time of Abram and Sarai, Canaan was primarily an agricultural society. Only later would the region develop a merchant class. Still, people traded products grown on their farms as well as animals from their flocks. In their local marketplaces, Abram and Sarai would have encountered locals trading wheat and barley, grapes and wine, olives and olive oil, figs, dates, and nuts, such as pistachios and almonds. Herders would have brought milk, cheese, and butter, and in late spring, they would have also brought young lambs and goats to market.

The Canaanites

The origin of the term *Canaan* is obscure. It was used in parts of Mesopotamia as a term for red or purple dye, a product for which the coastal Canaanites were famous. As a geographical designation, it was in use as early as the third millennium B.C.E. Biblical writers used "Canaanites" as a general description for inhabitants of Canaan. However, the people of Canaan were never united as a single nation, either ethnically or politically, although they shared similar cultures and languages. Canaan was made up of numerous city-states, many of which paid allegiance to foreign rulers, depending on which Egyptian or Mesopotamian empire was the strongest at a particular time.

44 *Abraham and Sarah*

Abram and Sarai are dressed like European pilgrims of the Middle Ages in this 14th-century Italian fresco depicting their journey to Canaan.

A Long, Difficult Journey

Abram and Sarai's journey south to Canaan was long and difficult. Abram, Sarai, and their family and followers were traveling on foot, driving their herds of livestock ahead of them. This was a slow and difficult way to travel, as robbers were a constant threat. So were wild animals. Though found mostly in the mountains of Lebanon today, the Syrian bear once roamed the entire area of Canaan. This light-colored bear liked to prey on sheep and goats. There were also wild goats in Canaan, as well as lions. References to lions are found in almost half of the books of the Bible. The biblical lion was smaller than the African lion and had a short curly mane. Still, it posed a serious threat to travelers on foot, who, on average, might walk about 20 miles per day.

Nomads were aided in their travels by pack animals like oxen and donkeys. Donkeys were used primarily to haul goods and plow fields, not carry people, though female donkeys were sometimes ridden by women, children, and people too sick to walk. Oxen pulled plows, threshed grain, and drew carts. People in Abram's time depended on these adult cattle the way modern farmers rely on tractors. And only wealthy people owned oxen, as they are large animals and need more and better pastures than goats or sheep.

In addition to the threats posed by robbers and wild animals, nomads faced another foe: insects. Insects are not to be taken lightly. Scientists have estimated that there are 800,000 kinds of insects on Earth, and they have been found almost everywhere since the beginning of time. Imagine walking hundreds of miles in extreme heat and humidity, dodging wild animals and robbers, only to find yourself attacked by bees, gnats, ants, flies, or spiders. Understanding the harsh conditions that Abram would have endured on his long journey to the Promised Land helps the modern reader better appreciate the strength of his character—physically, mentally, and spiritually.

ARRIVAL IN CANAAN

According to Genesis, Abram and Sarai travel south through Canaan to Shechem, a town located in a valley between the twin peaks of Mount Ebal and Mount Gerizim. (Shechem was located near the modern town of Nablus, in Israel.) It is here that God appears to Abram and confirmed that Canaan is indeed the land He will give to Abram's descendants, saying, "To your offspring I will give this land" (Genesis 12:6). To recognize and mark the

Several places where Abram and Sarai stopped on their journey through Canaan have been discovered and excavated. Shechem (above) is where Abram built an altar to the Lord, perhaps similar to the one standing on the right in this image. Ai (opposite page) was a fortified city believed to have been a ruin in Abram's time.

importance of this event, Abram builds his first altar to the Lord.

Abram does not remain in Shechem, however. He and Sarai continue their journey southward to an unnamed mountain between the towns of Bethel and Ai, where Abram builds a second altar and prays. Then Abram and Sarai resume their journey, continuing south toward the semiarid region of the Negev.

The Bible does not explain why Abram and Sarai continued traveling through Canaan. They may have been in search of more grazing lands for their animals. Abram and Sarai's large flocks included sheep, oxen, goats, donkeys, camels, and cattle. Animals are a nomad's wealth, and cattle, in particular, were a common form of money in biblical times. They were a unit of trade especially well suited for a pastoral, nomadic way of life. Herds such as Abram and Sarai's also provided their owners with meat, milk for drinking or butter, yogurt, and cheese, wool to be sold or woven into cloth for members of the household, skins for leather and the transportation of liquids, and dung for cooking fuel. They also provide acceptable sacrifices for God.

But a nomadic or even semi-nomadic life is by nature mobile, and mobility limits what a person can take along. No fixed residence means that a person is less likely to leave the traces that can tell those who come later how they lived. As a result, even what scholars think they know about Abram and Sarai's daily lives presents difficulties.

The common assumption, based on the account in Genesis and on the investigations and interpretations of scholars, has been that Abram was a very wealthy nomad and moved large flocks of animals throughout the land of Canaan sometime in the early part of the second millennium B.C.E. But historians such as John Van Seters, a noted scholar on the ancient Near East and the author of *Abraham in History and Tradition,* have pointed out serious problems with this portrayal of Abram's life. Genesis says that Abram owned many slaves, but Van Seters points out that this does not make sense. "Such a slavery-based economy is not part of the nomadic way of life because it has no need for a cheap labor force," he writes, "and there is nothing in the second millennium sources to suggest that nomads retained slaves as part of their social way of life."

According to Genesis 12:8, Abram makes his second stop in Canaan by a mountain between Bethel and Ai. Modern archaeological excavations suggest that the city of Ai was not occupied from 2400 to 1200 B.C.E., which would mean it was not a city during any possible dates that have been given for Abram's lifetime. This does not mean that the story in Genesis is inaccurate; in fact, it is interesting that the name *Ai* actually means "the ruin."

Even a detail as familiar to modern readers as the camel, often seen in depictions of Abram leaving Ur or traveling through Canaan, may be wrong. Archaeological and other evidence suggests that the camel was not fully domesticated or widely used as a working animal until centuries after the date generally given for Abram's lifetime.

Whatever the truth is, we cannot know for certain. But the explanation for Abram's continual movement is most likely found in verse 10 of Genesis 12: "Now there was a famine in the land." The next verse indicates that the famine was severe. Faced with a shortage of food and water for large numbers of people and animals, it is understandable that Abram and Sarai would continue on to a place where their household's survival would be more easily assured.

Abram and Sarai direct their herds south, toward Egypt, where there is a reliable source of abundant water from the Nile River, as well as lush grasslands that can be used for pasture. Egypt becomes a refuge for him, and by the time he departs, Abram will have accumulated even more wealth.

Travels and Travails

Abram's journey continues to unfold as a severe famine forces him to move southward through Canaan on to Egypt. But before he actually arrives in Egypt, Abram recognizes that there will be a problem once he reaches his destination: Sarai.

The first mention of Sarai, in Genesis 11, identifies her in two important ways: first as Abram's wife, and second as a woman who is infertile: "Now Sarai was barren; she had no children" (Genesis 11:30).

Despite her age, the Bible describes her as "beautiful," and apparently it was not uncommon in antiquity for powerful men to confiscate beautiful women. So Abram devises a plan to head off trouble:

> As he was about to enter Egypt, he said to his wife Sarai, "I know what a beautiful woman you are. When the Egyptians see you, they will say, 'This is his wife.' Then they will kill me but they will let

you live. Say you are my sister, so that I will be treated well for your sake and that my life will be spared because of you." (Genesis 12:11–13)

One rabbinical retelling of this story provides a more dramatic version. Before resorting to the lie that Sarai is his sister (she was, in fact, his half-sister), Abram hides her in a large chest, hoping to sneak her past the border guards of Egypt. But his negotiations do not go as well as he had planned. The guards see an opportunity to tax the

Enormous statues of Egyptian rulers flank the entrance to this ancient temple. In the time of Abraham, Egypt possessed the world's most advanced civilization and was a major world power.

newcomer, and ask to see the box's contents. Abram will not show them, and then things begin to go wrong:

> When he was come to the place of paying custom, the collectors said, 'Pay us the customs': and he said, 'I will pay the custom.' They said to him, 'Thou carriest clothes:' and he said, 'I will pay for clothes.' Then they said to him, 'Thou carriest gold:' and he answered them, 'I will pay for my gold.' On this they further said to him, 'Surely thou bearest the finest silk:' he replied, 'I will pay custom for the finest silk.' Then said the collectors, 'Surely it must be pearls that thou takest with thee:' and he only answered, 'I will pay for pearls.' Seeing that they could name nothing of value for which the patriarch was not willing to pay custom, they said, 'It cannot be but thou open the box, and let us see what is within.' So they opened the box, and the whole land of Egypt was illumined by the luster of Sarah's beauty,—far exceeding even that of pearls.

TROUBLE IN EGYPT

Abram was right to have expected trouble. When news of Sarai's great beauty reaches Pharaoh, the powerful ruler of Egypt takes her into his harem. Genesis is silent on Sarai's reaction. What is clear, however, is that Abram needs Sarai's cooperation, and he gets it. And not only is his life saved: he benefits economically as well. Pharaoh is apparently quite pleased with Sarai: "He treated Abram well for her sake, and Abram acquired sheep and cattle, male and female donkeys, menservants and maidservants, and camels" (Genesis 12:16).

But all is not well, and God intervenes. He afflicts Pharaoh and his household with diseases because of Sarai. Troubled, Pharaoh then calls to Abram, saying, "What

Sarai is presented to the Pharaoh, in this scene from the Bible of Borgo d'Este, an illuminated Italian manuscript of the 15th century.

have you done to me? Why didn't you tell me she was your wife? Why did you say, 'She is my sister,' so that I took her to be my wife? Now then, here is your wife. Take her and go!'" (Genesis 12:18–19).

Scholars have tried to find literary and legal explanations for Abram's deliberate lie. But no one has really

This Egyptian papyrus shows a pharaoh being attended to by several women.

succeeded in finding a completely satisfactory explanation for this behavior. Perhaps the real explanation for his actions may be much more practical and human than anyone might think. As Victor Matthews observed in *Manners and Customs in the Bible*:

> Another difficulty faced by every immigrant group arriving in a new land is legal helplessness. Immigrants are seldom familiar with the laws of the land and very often are not given the legal protections guaranteed to citizens. This can lead the immigrants to use deception as a defense mechanism. The morality of such a deception did not present a problem for the patriarchs since they assumed that their survival and that of their group had priority over providing a potential enemy with all the facts.

Forced to leave Egypt, Abram returns to Canaan with Sarai, Lot, his herds, servants, and their accumulated riches.

RETURN TO CANAAN

The third millennium was drawing to a close when Abram and Sarai arrived in Canaan for the second time. Urban life had been a feature of Canaanite culture. However, by the time Abram and Sarai arrived there from Egypt, things had changed. The population had moved from an agrarian

Cash Cows

The Bible says that Pharaoh gave cattle to Abram, thereby increasing his wealth. Cattle are still a measure of a man's wealth in parts of the world today, particularly in some parts of Africa where people maintain traditional lifestyles. A man who owns cattle, for example, is considered wealthier than a man who owns goats. As in most societies, wealthy people often command more respect and consideration than the poor, so it's to a person's advantage to acquire as many cattle as possible.

But cattle feature in the lives of not only rural people but also urban dwellers. For example, cattle are still used to pay lobola, or bride wealth, in South Africa. In 2007, the press there reported that the current Zulu king, Goodwill Zwelithini, received more than $40,000 along with 114 prized Nguni cattle from the man who married one of his princess daughters. Even former president Nelson Mandela reportedly paid 60 cattle for his third wife, Graca Michel.

Apparently, in South Africa the going rate for an average young woman is about 11 cows, which is quite a considerable expense for a young groom. Some grooms end up paying lobola well into their married life. Others are now using credit cards to pay. So a farmer with three daughters could receive enough to retire.

economy to one based on pastoral nomadism, so Abram would have fit in easily, grazing his flocks. Also, because Canaan was in a state of transition, disintegrating from an urban society to an agrarian land, Abram most likely would not have experienced problems with local kings, whose domains were limited geographically.

Although Abram would have enjoyed freedom of movement for his household and herds, he quickly realized that he and Lot owned too much livestock between them—there was insufficient grazing land to sustain them all. It is uncertain how many animals Abram might have owned, but the Bible says that he returned from Egypt "very wealthy in livestock and in silver and gold" (Genesis 13:2).

According to Jewish tradition, Lot's men have heard that God has told Abram that his descendants will receive the land that lies all about them. Because they believe Abram has no chance of producing an heir, they presume that their own master, Lot, will ultimately inherit the land. When Abram's herdsmen challenge them for allowing Lot's cattle to eat on land that is not their own—Abram has considerately muzzled his own cattle to prevent them from eating what is not theirs—Lot's herdsmen mockingly reply: "But Abram is a barren mule and cannot beget children. Soon he will die and his nephew Lot will be his heir. So if these cattle eat outside of Lot's fields, it is their own that they eat."

The situation is wisely resolved when Abram tells his nephew to choose land for himself.

> "Let's not have any quarreling between you and me, or between your herdsmen and mine, for we are brothers. Is not the whole land before you? Let's part company. If you go to the left, I'll go to the right; if you go to the right, I'll go to the left" (Genesis 13:8–9).

Given the opportunity to choose the best land, Lot decides to move eastward down into the Jordan River valley because it has plenty of water and good grazing areas. He and his family will later come to dwell among the cities of the valley, which include Sodom and Gomorrah.

According to Jewish tradition, Sodom may have been known for the immorality of its inhabitants, but it was also well known for its amazing natural wealth. One rabbinical commentator marvels that "there was not a path in Sodom that did not have the foliage of seven trees over it, each shading the one below it: foliage of the vine, fig, pomegranate, walnut and almond, apple, and peach, so that

The separation of Abram and Lot, from the Bible of Jean de Sy, circa 1355. Abram and Sarai are depicted together, while Lot drives his herds in the other direction.

"Lot looked up and saw that the whole plain of the Jordan was well watered, like the garden of the Lord, like the land of Egypt, toward Zoar. . . . So Lot chose for himself the whole plain of the Jordan and set out toward the east. The two men parted company: Abram lived in the land of Canaan, while Lot lived among the cities of the plain and pitched his tents near Sodom" (Genesis 13:10, 11–12). A modern view of the Jordan River valley.

each path was fully sheltered." Even the simple act of obtaining food for a daily meal could reveal the astonishing marvels of this land: "When a man would go to a gardener and say to him, 'Give me an issar's worth of greens,' and the gardener would rinse the greens in water, he would shake down gold flakes out of the soil clinging to their roots."

Finding the Canaan of Abram's Time

Although Genesis provides a detailed itinerary of Abram and Sarai's journeys, information presented in the

Scripture does not always match up with modern scientific research and scholarly opinion. While many of the places mentioned in the Bible are known because they have been continuously inhabited, or because they have been positively identified through archaeological excavations or contemporary documents, many problems and mysteries remain unresolved.

Even a location as seemingly well identified as Abraham's birthplace—"Ur of the Chaldees"—turns out to be uncertain, based on modern scholarship. In *Historical Atlas of the Holy Lands*, Karen Farrington explains:

> The Bible suggests it was Ur in present-day Iraq, which was indeed a thriving city even in those early times. But this may not be the correct Ur. Two other towns with similar names (Ura and Urfa) are to be found within the modern Turkish borders and both are within a short distance of Haran, the first place visited by Abraham, lying more than 1,000 miles distant from Ur.

It is certainly possible to learn a great deal about the land that Abram and Sarai would have seen and walked through. Though some 4,000 years have passed, that is just a moment in geologic time; the contours of hills, mountains, and valleys would not have changed dramatically in this time. But on a human scale, 4,000 years is an immense span of time. Small settlements grow into towns, which then grow into cities. Some cities thrive, but then—for reasons unknown to us—are abandoned for hundreds of years, and then are occupied once again. Other cities are sacked by enemies and razed to the ground, only to have a new city rise again upon the ruins, or even some miles away. If Abram and Sarai were to return today, the hills, valleys, and other features of the landscape might seem familiar to them; however, the human settlements they knew would no longer be recognizable.

The human settlements of ancient Canaan have been somewhat recovered through the work of archaeologists. There are hundreds of sites in Canaan known to have been settled in the second millennium B.C.E.; excavations at some of these sites, as well as at later ones, have revealed city walls and palaces, as well as humble rural homes and wells. Many sites have also yielded artifacts that range from the gold and jewelry worn by the wealthy to the clay pots and lamps used by the poor as they completed their daily chores. Even coprolites, the fossilized remains of human and animal feces, have provided exciting new information about what the ancient Canaanites ate and what parasites afflicted them. But even with all that is known about life as it might have been in Canaan, understanding Abram's lifestyle still presents exceptional challenges.

God's Covenant with Abram

After Lot's departure into the Jordan valley, the Lord again speaks to Abram: "Lift up your eyes from where you are and look north and south, east and west. All the land that you see I will give to you and your offspring forever" (Genesis 13:14–15). God then tells Abram to go forth and walk throughout this land, so once again Abram and Sarai journey southward with their household. On this journey, they stop at Hebron, where Abram builds another altar.

But all is not well. There are many small city-states in Canaan, with warring kings and shifting alliances. The Bible records one instance when the kings of five cities in the Valley of Siddim, which is located in the Dead Sea region, revolt against the rule of Chedorlaomer, king of Elam. Eventually Chedorlaomer leads a confederacy of allied armies from Mesopotamia in an

Mesopotamian warriors, relief sculpture from an ancient Assyrian palace. The Bible says that Chedorlaomer led his armies to the Valley of Siddim, an area believed to have been located at the southern end of the Dead Sea. This region is now covered by shallow waters.

attack against Sodom, Gomorrah, and the other three rebellious cities. The four Mesopotamian armies march south, where they are met by the armies of the rebellious kings. After an epic battle, the Canaanites are completely routed; the biblical narrator recounts that the Valley of Siddim is full of bitumen pits, and as the forces of the rebel kings flee for their lives to the mountains, some fall instead into these pits and perish. The triumphant forces

God's Covenant with Abram

of Chedorlaomer enter the defeated cities of Sodom and Gomorrah and seize all that they can, including Lot, his family, and all that he owns.

A man who has managed to escape the destruction makes his way to Abram and informs him of his nephew's fate. Abram gathers together 318 of his servants, as well as men from the nearby towns of Aner, Eshcol, and Mamre, and pursues the armies of the victorious kings northward to Dan, to the north of the Sea of Galilee. Then Abram proves himself both a warrior and a military strategist: he divides his men and makes a surprise attack under cover of night. The armies scatter before Abram and his men, who pursue them all the way to the north past Damascus. Abram's victory is complete: not only has he caused Chedorlaomer to flee for his life, he has stripped him of all his riches and he has safely rescued Lot, his household, and all his goods.

When Abram returns from his victory over the armies of Chedorlaomer, he experiences a strange encounter. Melchizedek, the king of Salem, emerges to greet the returning warrior. Melchizedek takes bread and wine to

> Bitumen is a sticky, semi-liquid substance similar to pitch or asphalt. It is a naturally occurring petroleum product that has been exposed to the processes of evaporation and oxidation, which make it very useful for waterproofing. In the ancient world it was extensively traded, and was used in activities such as shipbuilding, construction, and embalming. The *Moody Atlas of Bible Lands* notes, "It has been suggested that Cleopatra's desire to govern the Dead Sea region was stimulated by her eagerness to regulate bitumen trade."

Abram's weary troops, and he blesses Abram, saying:

> Blessed be Abram by God Most High,
> Creator of heaven and earth.
> And blessed be God Most High,
> who delivered your enemies into your hand (Genesis 14:19–20).

Abram, in return, gives Melchizedek a tenth of the booty seized from the rebel armies. This was later used to explain and justify the practice of tithing—the giving of a percentage (usually 10 percent) of one's income to support a religious organization like a Christian church or Jewish synagogue.

The victorious general next encounters Bera, the king of Sodom, who urges Abram to keep the loot taken in battle, but asks him to return the people to their kings and cities. But Abram's purpose was to rescue his kinsman Lot, which he has done, and he's not a greedy man interested only in acquiring personal wealth. He tells the king that he only wants to feed his soldiers and give them their fair share of the treasure; all the rest he will return. Abram does take the opportunity to attempt to introduce the polytheistic Bera to his all-powerful creator God, whom he credits as the source of all wealth and blessings. "I have raised my hand to the Lord, God Most High, Creator of

---

The conflict described in chapter 14 of Genesis is the first war recorded in biblical history. Nine nations were involved—led by four Mesopotamian kings and five Canaanite kings.

God's Covenant with Abram 65

The great 17th century Flemish artist Peter Paul Rubens painted this lush, sensual depiction of Abram's meeting with Melchizedek, the king of Salem. Abram is shown wearing armor resembling that of a soldier in the Roman empire.

heaven and earth, and have taken an oath that I will accept nothing belonging to you, not even a thread or the thong of a sandal, so that you will never be able to say, 'I made Abram rich,'" Abram tells Bera. "I will accept nothing but what my men have eaten and the share that belongs to the men who went with me—to Aner, Eshcol, and Mamre. Let them have their share" (Genesis 14:22–24).

THE FIRST COVENANT

After this great military victory, God appears again to Abram, this time in a vision, saying, "Do not be afraid,

"Then the word of the Lord came to [Abram]: "This man [Eliezer] will not be your heir, but a son coming from your own body will be your heir." He took him outside and said, "Look up at the heavens and count the stars—if indeed you can count them." Then He said to him, "So shall your offspring be" (Genesis 15:4–5).

Abram. I am your shield, your very great reward." (Genesis: 15:1).

Abram has shown great faith in the past, obeying God's commands without question and accepting his promises without need for assurances. But ten years have passed since he arrived in Canaan the first time, which is when God promised Abram an heir. Both Abram and Sarai are steadily growing older, and Abram wonders how the promise of posterity will come to pass, given the couples' ages.

When Abram questions God, his doubt is understandable. Abram points out that since he has no children, the one who will inherit all that he has and all that God has

God's Covenant with Abram

promised him is Eliezer of Damascus, a servant in Abram's household.

God assures Abram that he will have his own biological son. He further reiterates his promise to make him a father, of many, throughout time. "Look up at the heavens and count the stars—if indeed you can count them," God says. "So shall your offspring be" (Genesis 15:5).

Abram trusts God's word and is reassured. But then doubts return. This time Abram questions the promise that God seems already to have fulfilled—the promise of land. God provides Abram proof of his promises, but first He demands a sacrifice—a three-year-old heifer, a three-year-old ram, a turtledove, a three-year-old she-goat, and a young pigeon. When this is done, just at sunset, Abram falls into a sort of trance and God speaks to him about the future: his descendants will be strangers in a foreign land; they will be servants in that land, and their servitude will last for 400 years. But God himself will later judge the nation that enslaved Abram's descendants, and they will return to Canaan with great possessions. And Abram himself will live a long life and die in peace.

Then, in the darkness, God descends as fire over the sacrificed animals, and now makes his formal covenant with Abram, again reiterating his earlier promise in much greater detail. Now, instead of directing Abram to look toward all points of the compass, God tells Abram that his descendants will possess lands that stretch from the Nile to the river Euphrates, and he names all the tribes that will dwell therein. And so the first covenant is concluded.

Sarai's Plan

Sarai is just as concerned as Abram about the fact that they have no one to inherit their fortune. So she persuades Abram to take Hagar, her Egyptian slave, as a secondary wife so that she can have a child. Apparently, this practice was not uncommon in Abram's day; legally, Hagar's child would become Sarai's.

Abram agrees to his wife's wishes. Hagar conceives, but—knowing that her child will inherit Abram and Sarai's estate—she soon becomes arrogant. Angered, Sarai dismisses Hagar from the household, sending her away from the camp. But God sends his angel to Hagar, who has made her way to a spring in the wilderness. No doubt she is exhausted, hungry, and afraid. The angel commands Hagar to return to the house of her mistress.

Hagar obeys the angel, returning to the camp and reconciling with Sarai. She soon gives birth to a son, who is named Ishmael. At 86 years old, Abram has become the father of a son. If there is not complete harmony between the two women of Abram's household, at least there is not open enmity, and God promises to bless Ishmael.

Hagar's Background

Jewish and Islamic traditions provide information on Hagar's royal connections, which are not mentioned in Genesis. Legends say that she was the daughter of Pharaoh or of a high-ranking official in Egypt. When Abram and Sarai are expelled from Egypt, Hagar is given to Sarai as a handmaiden. Jewish legends relate that, because of Sarai's great virtue, Hagar's father believes his daughter will be better off even as a lowly slave in Sarai's household than as a princess in a great palace. Hagar herself may have felt somewhat differently; this could help explain why she comes to feel that she is better than her mistress when she becomes pregnant with Abram's first child.

It is interesting to note that Hagar is the first woman in the scriptures to whom God speaks directly.

God's Covenant with Abram 69

Guided by an angel, Hagar returns to the home of Abram and Sarai, where she will give birth to Abram's son Ishmael. This mid-17th century painting by Pietro da Cortona is on display at the Kunsthistorisches Museum in Vienna. In Genesis 16:12, the Angel of the Lord describes Ishmael's future to Hagar: "He will be a wild donkey of a man; his hand will be against everyone and everyone's hand against him, and he will live in hostility toward all his brothers."

So Ishmael grows up and is groomed to one day inherit Abram and Sarai's wealth, succeeding his father as head of the clan. Tradition says that he was an excellent hunter, although he was also something of a free spirit.

A Change in Plan

Sarai's plan is overturned when Ishmael is about 13 years old, however. In Genesis 17, God appears again to 99-year-old Abram, commanding him to circumcise himself, along with all the males of his household; future males born into his family must be circumcised on the eighth day after their birth. God also changes his faithful servant's name from Abram (which means "exalted father" in Hebrew) to Abraham ("father of many nations"), for He promises:

> I will make you very fruitful; I will make nations of you, and kings will come from you. I will establish my covenant as an everlasting covenant between me and you and your descendants after you for the generations to come, to be your God and the God of your descendants after you. The whole land of Canaan, where you are now an alien, I will give as an everlasting possession to you and your descendants after you; and I will be their God (Genesis 17:6–8).

> Depending on the translation or commentary, many different terms are used to describe Hagar: maid, handmaiden, servant, slave, wife, concubine. The specific term is not as important as is the concept that she had a lower social status in Abraham's household.

What's in a Name?

Why are Abram and Sarai's names changed? The changes seem minimal: what difference can one or two letters make? But they *do* make a difference, and here is why: in addition to the subtle change in meaning in Abraham's role as a father, the added *h* (the Hebrew letter *heh*) brings something exceptionally special with it, explain psychologists Gustav Dreifuss and Judith Riemer in *Abraham: The Man and the Symbol*:

> *h* signifies God, since the Hebrew letter *heh* often serves as an abbreviation for the name of God. Thus God enters Abraham's innermost being—his Self—endowing him with some of his own power and making himself an inseparable part of Abraham's being, the Self. Thus Abraham becomes the living message identified with God.

Sarai's name too will change, to Sarah. And with this change comes the announcement that she will give birth to a son, Isaac. According to the Genesis account, God declares that this son shall become Abraham's heir: Isaac will be the one whose descendants become God's "chosen people." God promises Abraham, "I will establish my covenant with [Isaac] as an everlasting covenant for his descendants after him. And as for Ishmael . . . I will surely bless him; I will make him fruitful and will greatly increase his numbers. He will be the father of twelve rulers, and I will make him into a great nation. But my covenant I will establish with Isaac, whom Sarah will bear to you by this time next year."

6

THE PROMISED CHILD

Soon after God makes his second covenant with Abraham, three "men" appear at the patriarch's encampment, on their way to investigate rumors about the sinfulness of the inhabitants of Sodom and Gomorrah.

Abraham is resting in his tent at the hottest part of the day when the three suddenly appear before him. He rises to his feet, then bows down before them. He next offers water so that they can wash the dust of their journey from their feet, and bids them rest in the shade of a tree. He brings them bread, and as his guests rest and refresh themselves, Abraham finds Sarah and tells her to prepare cakes of fine flour with her own hands; he then selects a tender young calf from his herds, and brings it to a servant to prepare. In Abraham's time, the calf was considered the choicest of all meats, and was reserved for festive or special occasions.

Hospitality was one of the most highly praised virtues in antiquity. Some legends tell of how Abraham was the proprietor of an inn, others of how he welcomed travelers and townspeople alike: "Our father Abraham would bring people into his home, give them food and drink, befriend them, and thus attract them, and then convert them and bring them under the wings of the Presence."

Abraham lays out a feast for the three visitors. He places meat, milk, and *chemal* before his guests. *Chemal* is a Hebrew term, variously translated as cream, curds, cheese, or butter.

The Bible eventually identifies the three "men" as angels; one is, in fact, the "Angel of God." The Angel of God warns Abraham that he is about to destroy Sodom.

Abraham entertains the three angels, while Sarah watches from another room, in this 17th-century painting by the Dutch master Rembrandt. When Sarah hears an angel tell Abraham that they will have a child, she cannot help but laugh.

> The Angel of the Lord is understood to be God himself. The angel appears eight times to different people in the Old Testament, starting with Hagar, after she fled into the desert. He also appears to Abraham, Jacob, and Moses, among others.

But Abraham is horrified, and asks God to spare the city on behalf of the righteous people he believes are living there—including his nephew, Lot. "Will you sweep away the righteous with the wicked?" Abraham asks God in Genesis 18:23–25. "What if there are fifty righteous people in the city? Will you really sweep it away and not spare the place for the sake of the fifty righteous people in it? Far be it from you to do such a thing—to kill the righteous with the wicked, treating the righteous and the wicked alike. Far be it from you! Will not the Judge of all the earth do right?"

God, in a concession to his faithful friend, agrees not to destroy the city if 50 righteous men can be found. But, Abraham continues, what if there are only 45? God accepts this number as well. And so Abraham continues haggling downward until they reach the figure 10: if this number of righteous men is found in the city, promises God, he will not destroy the city.

In the meantime, the two angels have already set out for Sodom. While Abraham negotiates with God, the two angels arrive in Sodom. There, the angels are met by Lot, who invites them into his home.

The men of the city, true to their wicked reputation, surround Lot's house and demand that he hand over his guests to them. "Where are the men who came to you tonight?" they call to Lot. "Bring them out to us so that we can have sex with them" (Genesis 19:5). Lot comes out of his house, shuts the door, tries to reason with the angry mob, and when they do not listen, offers his two virgin daughters in place of his guests.

The mob is not placated by Lot's offer. Menacingly, they draw near to break down Lot's door and seize the two travelers. But the angels "reached out and pulled Lot back into the house and shut the door. Then they struck the men who were at the door of the house, young and old, with blindness so that they could not find the door" (Genesis 19:10–11).

This incident proves that there are not even 10 righteous people in Sodom, as Abraham had hoped, and so God destroys the city. But he spares Lot, his wife, and their two daughters. The angels guide them out of the city, before it is consumed. According to the Bible, however, Lot's wife turns back to watch fire and brimstone rain

This French painting shows two angels hovering over the doomed city of Gomorrah. Genesis 19:24–25 describes the destruction of the wicked cities in this way: "Then the Lord rained down burning sulfur on Sodom and Gomorrah—from the Lord out of the heavens. Thus he overthrew those cities and the entire plain, including all those living in the cities—and also the vegetation in the land."

The Lost Cities of Canaan

One of the most fascinating mysteries in Genesis involves the destruction of Sodom and Gomorrah, two cities known in the Bible for the wickedness of their inhabitants. Beginning in the 17th century, some people began to doubt that Sodom and Gomorrah had ever existed at all. These people argued that the tale of Sodom and Gomorrah had been created to warn people about the consequences of sin and immorality.

Modern scholars have determined that the cities probably did exist in Abraham's time. They were probably located in the vicinity of the Dead Sea, the lowest point on earth. Cemeteries dating from as early as 3200 B.C.E. have been discovered in that area. However, archaeologists are not certain exactly where Sodom and Gomorrah were located. Some scholars believe these cities lay to the north of the Dead Sea, while others think they were located to the south.

"For years the tale of Sodom and Gomorrah appeared metaphorical, a dire warning about the consequences of immorality," writes Karen Farrington in *Historical Atlas of the Holy Lands*. "Now it seems the cities probably did exist and were swallowed up by an earthquake in about 1900 B.C., although some experts date the seismic eruptions at some four centuries prior. Oil and gases occurring naturally in the region would have ignited, causing colossal explosions and perhaps a firestorm like that related in Genesis. Afterward, the waters of the Dead Sea closed over the sites."

Lot and his family flee from Sodom, in an illustration by Gustave Doré.

down on the city, and when she does, she is changed into a "pillar of salt."

THE BIRTH OF ISAAC

Fourteen years after the birth of Ishmael, Abraham's son by the Egyptian servant, Sarah gives birth to Isaac. When God had originally announced to Abraham and Sarah that she would give birth to a son, Genesis 17:17 says the couple laughed: "Will a son be born to a man a hundred years old? Will Sarah bear a child at the age of ninety?" But God fulfills his promise, and Abraham and Sarah name their son Isaac, which means "laughter." Abraham and Sarah live up to their part of the covenant, and circumcise the infant when he is eight days old.

Two or three years later, Isaac is weaned, and Abraham prepares a great feast to celebrate the occasion. All seems well, but Sarah notices that Ishmael mocks Isaac. Sarah becomes angry and insists that Abraham drive Hagar and her son out of the household. Sarah is no doubt jealous and concerned about Ishmael's claim to her husband's legacy. "Get rid of that slave woman and her son," she says, "for that slave woman's son will never share in the inheritance with my son Isaac" (Genesis 21:10).

> According to Jewish tradition, God rejuvenates Sarah's aged body so that she will be fully prepared physically to conceive and give birth. Some legends even tackle the doubts of neighbors, who cannot believe that Isaac is actually the couple's biological child. To test Sarah, the women bring their babies to her to nurse; Sarah easily produces enough milk to satisfy the hunger of all the infants.

A jealous Sarah watches from the doorway, with Isaac at her skirts, as Abraham banishes Hagar and Ishmael from their home. This 17th-century Dutch painting contains numerous inaccuracies—Ishmael appears to be about 5 or 6, instead of a teenager as the Bible indicates; Abraham and Sarah live in a house rather than a tent; and all of the figures wear clothing that would have been commonplace during the artist's lifetime, but not in Abraham's. However, the artist does capture Abraham's emotional torment as he is forced to banish his oldest child, as well as Hagar's anxiety at being thrust into the wilderness with her young son.

According to the culture of the period and the region, as Abraham's firstborn son Ishmael should inherit a larger share of his father's estate. Typically, the older brother's inheritance would be twice as much as the younger brother's share. But Ishmael is also the son of a foreign woman, a woman much lower in social status than Sarah.

At first Abraham is reluctant. It is clear in the Bible that he loves his older son; in Genesis 17:18, when God promises that Sarah will bear a child who will become his heir, Abraham's first reaction is to ask that Ishmael not lose his favored status as the firstborn: "If only Ishmael might live under your blessing!" But God intervenes on Sarah's side, telling Abraham, "Do not be so distressed about the boy and your maidservant. Listen to whatever Sarah tells you, because it is through Isaac that your offspring will be reckoned" (Genesis 21:12). So Abraham gets up early the next morning, takes a skin filled with water and some bread, gives them to Hagar, and then sends her and their son out of the camp and into the wilderness. The Bible does not explicitly say what

Rights of the Firstborn Son

According to the Bible, hundreds of years after the death of Abraham and Sarah God gave a complex set of laws and guidelines for daily life to Moses. These laws are preserved in the Torah, particularly the books of Exodus, Leviticus, and Deuteronomy. Deuteronomy 21:15-17 spells out the rights of the oldest son to inherit a larger portion of his father's estate:

> If a man has two wives, and he loves one but not the other, and both bear him sons but the firstborn is the son of the wife he does not love, when he wills his property to his sons, he must not give the rights of the firstborn to the son of the wife he loves in preference to his actual firstborn, the son of the wife he does not love. He must acknowledge the son of his unloved wife as the firstborn by giving him a double share of all he has. That son is the first sign of his father's strength. The right of the firstborn belongs to him.

Abraham expected Hagar and Ishmael to do once they left the camp. However, an experienced nomad would have understood that this small amount of food and water would not sustain a woman and child for long in the dry and barren land of the Negev.

THE LIFE OF ISHMAEL

The situation in which Hagar and Ishmael now find themselves seems desperate. Water is scarce in the wilderness; without an adequate supply or without knowledge of what springs and wells are located in the area, travel becomes extremely hazardous. Soon Hagar and Ishmael are alone, the water skin is empty, and no water is in sight. Hagar places her son under a bush—perhaps in a last, desperate attempt to give him a moment of comfort—and sits down some distance away from him, so that she will not have to watch her child die from thirst.

At this moment Ishmael cries; the Lord hears him, and speaks to Hagar, telling her not to despair. As she opens her eyes, a spring of fresh water appears, and mother and child are saved. Genesis 21:20–21 explains, "God was with the boy as he grew up. He lived in the desert and became an archer. While he was living in the Desert of Paran, his mother got a wife for him from Egypt."

At this point, Ishmael and Hagar pass out of the biblical story—as far as Jews and Christians are concerned, Abraham never sees his oldest son again, although Ishmael does return to bury his father with Isaac when Abraham dies (a story recounted in Genesis 25). The Islamic account of Ishmael's life is significantly different, however. According to Muslim traditions, Abraham does not expel Ishmael and Hagar into the wilderness. Instead, he travels with them to Mecca, a city on the Arabian Peninsula. When they arrive, Abraham and Ishmael work together to rebuild the Kaaba, a square building that Muslims consider God's house on Earth. (Islamic legend holds that the Kaaba was originally built by Adam, the first man; Muslims consider it the holiest religious shrine and the center of the world.) Outside the Kaaba is a stone known as the Maqam Ibrahim (the Station of Abraham), which is said to bear Abraham's footprint. According to Muslim tradition, Ishmael moved this stone from place to place for his father to stand on as he raised the walls of the Kaaba.

In another story, versions of which are found in both Jewish and Islamic folktales, Abraham sets out to visit Ishmael in the wilderness after promising Sarah that he

Muslim pilgrims circle the Kaaba, an ancient square building located in the center of the Grand Mosque of Mecca, during the annual ritual pilgrimage called the Hajj. The Kaaba is the holiest shrine in Islam; Muslims believe it was originally built by Adam, the first man, and that Abraham and Ishmael rebuilt the Kaaba after it had been damaged by Noah's Flood.

will not get down from his camel when he arrives. At Ishmael's house, Abraham finds his son's wife home alone. Abraham does not tell her his name, and instead asks for refreshment after his long journey. She refuses; Abraham gives her a rather cryptic message for Ishmael and departs.

Upon arriving home, Ishmael hears the message and promptly divorces his wife, whereupon his mother finds him another, this time from her own family in Egypt. The same scene is later repeated, but this time the new wife feeds the weary traveler. As a reward for her hospitality, Abraham asks that God fill his son's house with "all manner of good things."

Genesis 25 agrees that God lives up to the promises he made to Abraham and Hagar. Ishmael does become a great nation, fathering 12 sons before dying at the age of 137; the numerous descendants of Ishmael's sons multiply and form various Arab tribes. The Bible says these Ishmaelites "settled in the area from Havilah to Shur, near the border of Egypt, as you go toward Asshur. And they lived in hostility toward all their brothers" (Genesis 25:18). Centuries later, Ishmael's most famous descendant will be born: the Prophet Muhammad, who will preach the messages that will become the religion of Islam.

A Second Act of Deception

Sometime between the time of the announcement of Isaac's birth and the birth itself, Abraham moves into the land of the Philistines. There, he gets caught up in another act of deception, this time with Abimelech, the king of Gerar, a city west of Beersheba.

Abraham tells Abimelech that Sarah is his sister, just as he had previously lied to Pharaoh in Egypt. Some 25 years have passed since that incident in Egypt. But this time God himself appears to Abimelech in a dream, warning him: "You are as good as dead because of the woman you have taken; she is a married woman" (Genesis 20:3). Abimelech, justifiably upset, protests that he is an innocent man, having believed the words of both Abraham and Sarah. God acknowledges the truth of the king's words and urges him to return Sarah to Abraham, so that the king's life may be spared. Abimelech calls Abraham to him, saying in Genesis 20:9–10: "What have you done to us? How have I wronged you that you have brought such great guilt upon me and my kingdom? You have done things to me that should not be done. . . . What was your reason for doing this?"

Abraham blames his actions on fear. Sarah is returned to Abraham, and Abimelech sends him away with sheep, oxen, male and female servants, as well as a thousand pieces of silver. In addition, Abraham is invited to dwell in the king's land wherever he would like. Abraham then prays for God to bless Abimelech.

A Peace Treaty

This is not the last time that Abraham and Abimelech have dealings with each other. One day Abraham tells Abimelech that some of his servants have taken over one

---

When Abimelech paid Abraham a thousand silver shekels, he did not give him coins. Abimelech gave pieces of silver that weighed a shekel each. The shekel was the common unit of weight in the ancient Middle East. Modern biblical scholars estimate that a thousand shekels of silver would have weighed about 25 pounds (11.5 kg).

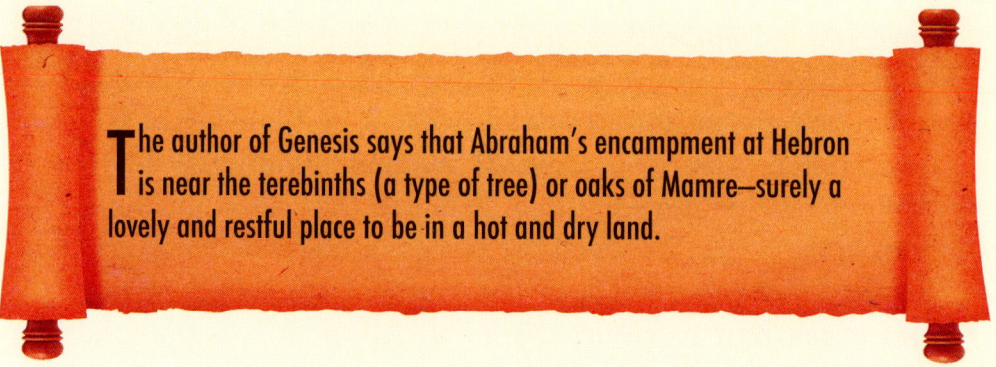

The author of Genesis says that Abraham's encampment at Hebron is near the terebinths (a type of tree) or oaks of Mamre—surely a lovely and restful place to be in a hot and dry land.

of his wells. Abimelech is unaware of the situation, but does not want trouble. He recognizes that God blesses everything that Abraham does, so he says to the patriarch, "Now swear to me here before God that you will not deal falsely with me or my children or my descendants. Show to me and the country where you are living as an alien the same kindness I have shown to you" (Genesis 21:23).

Abraham promises, then gives Abimelech seven female lambs from his flock. "Accept these seven lambs from my hand as a witness that I dug this well," Abraham tells him (Genesis 21:30). Abimelech accepts the lambs, and the place is named Beersheba, which means "well of oaths." Abraham then plants a tamarisk tree in Beersheba, and prays to God.

The Ultimate Test

In one last test of faith, God directs Abraham to offer up his son as a human sacrifice: "Take your son, your only son Isaac, whom you love, and go to the land of Moriah, and offer him there as a burnt offering upon one of the mountains of which I shall tell you" (Genesis 22:2).

Abraham obeys: he rises early in the morning to make preparations for the trip, saddling the donkey, cutting wood for the fire on the altar, and readying Isaac and two young men of his household, who will accompany them. On the third day of their journey, Abraham sees the place that God has designated for Isaac's sacrifice far off in the distance. He tells the two young men to wait with the donkey; he and Isaac will go off and worship, and then return.

Isaac notices that there is no lamb for the sacrifice. Abraham replies that God will provide a sacrifice. So Abraham builds the altar, lays the wood upon it, ties up Isaac, and places him upon the wood.

Genesis 22:5 refers to Isaac as a "boy." However, biblical scholars have placed him anywhere in age from a very young child to a 37-year-old man, and artistic depictions of this event have done the same. Both of the paintings on these pages were painted in the mid-17th century and are titled "The Sacrifice of Isaac." Jan Lievens the Elder's painting (above) presents a younger Isaac, while Agostino Beltrano's (opposite) depicts Isaac as a teenager.

Then he takes the knife in his hand. But before he can slay Isaac, the Lord stops Abraham: "Do not lay a hand on the boy," God says. "Do not do anything to him. Now I know that you fear God, because you have not withheld from me your son, your only son" (Genesis 22:12).

Abraham looks around and notices that a ram has become entangled in a nearby thicket; it is this animal that becomes the sacrifice. Abraham and Isaac then descend the mountain to where the two young men of Abraham's household have been waiting, and together all journey to Beersheba, in the Negev. And once again God spells out Abraham's reward for his faith: blessings for him and his descendants, who will increase so much that no man will be able to count their number.

Muslims agree that this event testing Abraham's commitment to God did take place; however, according to Islamic tradition, it is Ishmael, not Isaac, that Abraham was commanded to sacrifice. According to the Qur'an,

Abraham says to Ishmael beforehand, "My son, I see in a dream that I am sacrificing you. What do you think?" Ishmael replies, "O my father, do what you are commanded to do. You will find me, God willing, patient" (Qur'an 37:102). After God sees that both Abraham and Ishmael are willing to submit to His will, and He stops the sacrifice from proceeding, the Qur'an comments on Abraham's faith. "We thus reward the righteous. That was an exacting test indeed. We ransomed [Ishmael] by substituting an animal sacrifice. And we preserved his history for subsequent generations. Peace be upon Abraham. . . . He is one of our believing servants" (Qur'an 37:105–109, 111).

Symbol of Faith

The binding of Isaac—or Ishmael, depending upon which tradition one follows—is the ultimate act of loyalty and cements Abraham's relationship with God. Up until this point, Abraham has questioned God's judgment at times; in other cases, he leans on his own understanding, which in every instance gets him in trouble. But here we see that Abraham's faith is so strong, after enduring a famine, winning a war, and fathering a son at the age of 100, that he fully submits to the will of God.

> Some scholars have speculated that the story of Abraham being ordered to sacrifice his son may be related to practices that occurred among the native Canaanite populations. For example, at least two groups of people living in Canaan—the Moabites and Ammonites—are known to have sacrificed children to their gods Chemosh and Molech by throwing them into a fire.

Legends about the Binding

Jewish scholars have their own interpretation of why God tested Abraham in this way—they blame Satan. After the great feast that Abraham prepared for the weaning of Isaac, Satan remarks that Abraham, whom God so blessed by giving him a son at such an advanced age, has forgotten from whom this blessing has come. According to this legend, Abraham's attention is so focused on Isaac that, Satan claims, he has not even bothered to offer so much as one tiny bird to God.

God responds to Satan, "Is it not true that Abraham prepared the feast in honor of his son? Still, if I say to him, 'Sacrifice your son to Me,' he will sacrifice him at once." Satan then responds to God: "Try him." So God decides to indeed test Abraham. But Abraham reminds God that he has two sons, by two different mothers, and he cannot pick the one he loves most, for he loves both equally. Thus it is God who decides—for reasons unexplained in the folk tale—that it is Isaac who will be sacrificed.

Another legend describes how Abraham explains to Sarah why he is taking their young son into the wilderness: "Abraham said to Sarah, 'You know, when I was only three years old, I became aware of my Maker, but this lad, growing up, has not yet been taught [about his Creator]. Now, there is a place far away where youngsters are taught [about Him]. Let me take him there.'" Sarah agrees, and Abraham sets off very early the next morning so that his wife will not have an opportunity to change her mind.

Author Bruce Feiler, a journalist who has traveled extensively in the region in a metaphorical search for Abraham, has this to say:

> The binding of Abraham's favored son is the most celebrated episode in the patriarch's life. All three religions hail it as the ultimate expression of Abraham's relationship with God. But what the incident actually says, where it took place, even which son is involved are matters of centuries-old dispute. All this makes the binding the most debated, the most misunderstood, and the most combustible event in the entire Abraham story.

As Feiler notes in a recent biography, the story of Abraham's willingness to sacrifice his son in obedience to God's command presents Jews, Christians, and Muslims with a powerful symbol of faith and personal sacrifice in the face of suffering. "Abraham is a true believer, who submits to God's will, however extreme, and is rewarded for his efforts," writes Feiler in *Abraham: A Journey to the Heart of Three Faiths*. "God wants all humans to sacrifice our profane desires—even parental love—to serve a higher calling."

THE DEATH OF SARAH

In Genesis 23, Sarah dies at the age of 127. Isaac is 37, and Abraham is 137. He returns to Hebron to weep over her death and make plans for her burial.

A Hittite named Ephron sells Abraham the cave of Machpelah as a burial place for Sarah. Abraham pays 400 shekels of silver for the cave, purchasing the entire field in which it is located. The site traditionally believed to be the cave of Machpelah is located in the modern town of Hebron, and is known today as the Tomb of the

The Ultimate Test

This Islamic illustration depicts Abraham preparing to sacrifice his son, while an angel provides an alternate sacrifice. All of the figures have distinctly Asian features.

Patriarchs. A mosque now stands over the ancient burial site; little is really known of the cave beyond what tradition tells us.

The choice of such a specific location has been of great interest to commentators, who felt that Abraham must have had a good reason for choosing it. According to Jewish tradition, Abraham had previously discovered this cave at the time the three angels visited him on their way to Sodom. In that rabbinical story, Abraham selects a calf to prepare for God and the angels. The little calf runs away from Abraham, who follows it into the cave of Machpelah. "When Abraham entered after it, he saw Adam and his mate lying asleep on couches, lamps burning above them, and their bodies giving forth a goodly

In Gustave Doré's illustration of Sarah's burial, Abraham turns back for a final adoring look at the woman with whom he has spent a lifetime in service to God.

odor, sweet in savor," the tale goes. Since Abraham is a direct descendant of Adam, he believes that this will be the perfect burial site.

A Wife for Isaac

Three years after Sarah's death, Abraham searches for a wife for Isaac. He does not want Isaac to marry a woman from Canaan; instead, he decides to find a wife from among his kinsmen. Abraham calls his oldest, most trusted servant to him—probably Eliezer of Damascus—and tells him to return to Haran, where Abraham's family still lives, and to choose a wife for Isaac from among the women there. The servant departs with 10 of his master's camels, "taking with him all kinds of good things from his master" (Genesis: 24:10).

When the servant arrives in Haran, he lets the camels kneel down to rest near a well. It is evening, when women typically go out to draw water. Then the servant starts to pray:

> O Lord, God of my master Abraham, give me success today, and show kindness to my master Abraham. See, I am standing beside this spring, and the daughters of the townspeople are coming out to draw water. May it be that when I say to a girl, "Please let down your jar that I may have a drink," and she says, "Drink, and I'll water your camels too"—let her be the one you have chosen for your servant Isaac. By this I will know that you have shown kindness to my master. (Genesis 24:12–14).

Before the servant even finishes praying, a young woman named Rebekah appears and offers water to Abraham's servant and to his camels. Rebekah then takes

"All the damsels said they could not give [Eliezer] of their water, because they had to take it home," records one Jewish Midrash that elaborates on Eliezer's wait at the well in Haran. *"Then appeared Rebekah, coming to the well contrary to her wont, for she was the daughter of a king. . . . When Eliezer addressed his request for water to drink to this young innocent child, not only was she ready to do his bidding, but she rebuked the other maidens on account of their discourtesy to a stranger."* This 1701 painting of the scene hangs in the Louvre, Paris.

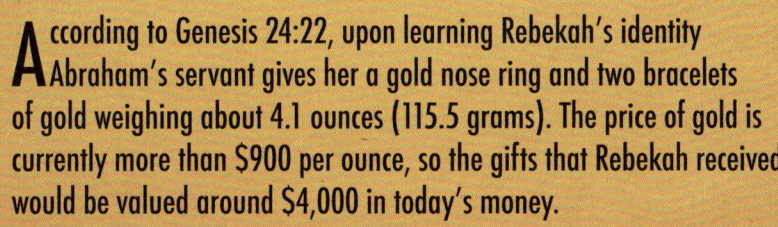

According to Genesis 24:22, upon learning Rebekah's identity Abraham's servant gives her a gold nose ring and two bracelets of gold weighing about 4.1 ounces (115.5 grams). The price of gold is currently more than $900 per ounce, so the gifts that Rebekah received would be valued around $4,000 in today's money.

the servant to meet her family; it turns out that her grandfather, a man named Nahor, is Abraham's older brother.

Rebekah's father, Bethuel, agrees to let Eliezer take her back to Abraham's camp in Canaan, where she will be married to Isaac. Gifts of silver and gold jewelry and other objects of great value are exchanged, and then the party of travelers sets out on the long journey home to Canaan.

Isaac is out walking in the fields in the evening, thinking, when he sees the caravan in the distance. Rebekah, too, sees Isaac, and asks the servant who he is; she waits, her veil covering her face, until the servant has given the report of his journey to Isaac. Genesis 24:67 reports, "Isaac brought her into the tent of his mother Sarah, and he married Rebekah. So she became his wife, and he loved her; and Isaac was comforted after his mother's death."

Abraham's Last Days

Abraham, too, finds comfort. He takes another wife, Keturah, who bears him six more sons: Zimran, Jokshan, Medan, Midian, Ishbak, and Shuah. All of these men, according to tradition, become the ancestors of various Semitic tribes. Nothing is known of Keturah's fate, but

> Some scholars have claimed that Keturah is really Hagar, returned to Abraham's favor after Sarah's death. If nothing else, that's an interesting twist to the story.

according to the Bible, Abraham gave each of his sons gifts before his death. However, the Bible notes that Abraham sent Ishmael and his six sons by Keturah to live in the east, far from Isaac, to whom Abraham left the balance of his possessions.

Abraham lives for 38 years after Sarah's death, dying at the age of 175. His passing is described in Genesis 25:8: "Then Abraham breathed his last and died at a good old age, an old man and full of years; and he was gathered to his people." His son Ishmael returns to Hebron, helping Isaac to bury Abraham in the tomb at the cave of Machpelah.

Patriarch of Many Nations

During Abraham's long life, his faith is tested many times. When faced with crises, he doesn't always make good choices. Nevertheless, he proves that he is willing to be different, willing to make sacrifices; he is both courageous and humble, and possesses a strong sense of justice. Abraham also is a strong leader and mediator who, with God's help, maintains order in volatile situations.

The Blessings of Abraham

Most of all, Abraham learns what it means to have faith: he learns to put all his trust in God, so much so that when God asks him to sacrifice his son, he obeys. Theirs is a two-way relationship—God reaching out to Abraham and Abraham reaching out to God. And because of Abraham's faith, God, the possessor of heaven and Earth, guarantees his success in all things and supplies all his needs, in abundance: land, silver and gold, servants, large herds of cattle and livestock, protection from his enemies, long life, and heirs. Genesis 24:1, 35 describe God's blessings in this way:

> Abraham was now old and well advanced in years, and the Lord had blessed him in every way.... The Lord has blessed [Abraham] abundantly, and he has become wealthy. He has given him sheep and cattle, silver and gold, menservants and maidservants, and camels and donkeys.

Only once in the biblical narrative do we read that Abraham provides for his own needs, and that is when he pays 400 shekels to buy land to bury his wife. Otherwise, Abraham is always receiving—either gifts from kings or blessings from God.

Abraham is an extraordinary figure. Walking with him through the Bible, the modern reader experiences the drama of his long life—a life in which good trumps evil, justice prevails over injustice, mercy beats out malice, right wins against wrong, and, most important of all, disobedience bows in submission to obedience.

The moment in which Abraham submits to God and shows himself willing to sacrifice his son stands as an ultimate act of faith for Christians, Jews, and Muslims. The Muslims call what Abraham did *aslama* ("to submit"), and reenact the event during one of the most sacred festivals of their calendar, Eid al-Adha (the Feast of the Sacrifice). This takes place at the end of the Hajj, a ritual pilgrimage to Mecca that every Muslim is expected to make at least once during his or her lifetime. Jews refer to it as *t'shuva*, which means "turning toward God," and recite Genesis 22 at their annual services for Rosh Hoshanah. For

During Rosh Hoshanah services, a ram's horn (shofar, pictured above) is sounded to remind Jews of the ram that Abraham sacrificed in place of his son Isaac.

Christians, the story prefigures the Crucifixion, when God the Father sacrifices his only son, Jesus.

TRUTH OR FICTION?

Genesis and other stories about Abraham and Sarah create a very detailed world, but scholars continue to debate the accuracy of these stories. Some details described in the Bible, such as the offering of hospitality to travelers, match what archaeologists and scientists have learned about life in Canaan and in the Middle East 4,000 years ago. Other details, like the slaves and servants who were

This building stands over the ancient cave tomb where Abraham and Sarah are believed to have been buried. Jews, Christians, and Muslims consider the Cave of the Patriarchs a holy site.

purportedly part of Abraham and Sarah's household, seem more debatable.

Ultimately, trying to reconstruct the daily life of people who lived a nomadic lifestyle some 4,000 years ago is extremely difficult, if not impossible. Scholars and theologians will no doubt continue attempting to learn more about Abraham and Sarah. But as for Abraham's devout "children"—Christians, Jews, and Muslims—there is one point on which they can all agree: Abraham was truly a man of God: faithful, obedient, hospitable, prayerful, and a man of extreme generosity. And for these qualities, God richly blessed him.

Notable Figures

Abimelech: The Philistine king of Gerar. Led to believe that Sarah was Abraham's sister, he took her into his house, but when he found out otherwise, he returned her to Abraham and compensated him handsomely.

Abraham: A God-fearing man, typically considered the first monotheist and revered by Jews, Christians, and Muslims. Abraham's descendants include the Jews (from the line of his second son, Isaac) and the Arabs (from his older son, Ishmael, as well as the six sons borne to him by Keturah).

Adam: The first man, made out of the dust of the earth. His sin causes a curse to fall upon all people.

Bera: A king of Sodom during the time of Abraham.

Chedorlaomer: A king of Elam who waged war against Sodom and Gomorrah, but was defeated by Abraham.

Eliezer: Abraham's chief servant.

Eve: The first woman; wife of Adam. She was made from one of her husband's ribs.

Hagar: Sarah's Egyptian servant, who gives birth to Abraham's son, Ishmael. At Sarah's insistence, Abraham eventually drives Hagar away from their camp.

Haran: A brother of Abraham who died before his father.

Isaac: The son of Abraham and Sarah, from whom the Jewish people are said to be descended.

Ishmael: The son of Abraham and Hagar; ancestor of the Arabs.

Keturah: Abraham's wife after the death of Sarah. She gives birth to six sons; Abraham gives each of them presents, but does not allow them to live near Isaac.

Lot: Abraham's nephew, the son of Abraham's brother Haran. He was taken captive by forces led by Chedorlaomer, but was freed by Abraham's forces. Later, he escaped with most of his family from Sodom just before it was destroyed.

Melchizedek: the king of Salem (Jerusalem) and priest of the Most High God, who blesses Abraham after he defeats the four kings of Mesopotamia.

Nahor: a son of Terah and the older brother of Abraham. His granddaughter, Rebekah, becomes Abraham's son Isaac's wife.

Nimrod: a Mesopotamian king who seeks to kill Abraham.

Noah: The hero of the biblical flood, which God sent to kill every living thing on Earth, except Noah, his family, and the animals that lived on the boat with him.

Pharaoh: the ruler of Egypt, who takes Sarah into his household believing she is Abraham's sister. As punishment, God sends a plague to trouble Pharaoh until he asks forgiveness, gives Abraham rich gifts, and asks him to leave Egypt.

Rebekah: the daughter of Bethuel, who passes the test at the well posed by Abraham's servant and becomes Isaac's wife.

Sarah: The wife of Abraham, who gives birth to a son, Isaac, when she is 90 years old.

Terah: the father of Abraham, who lives to be 205 years old.

Notes

CHAPTER 2: GOD CALLS ABRAM

p. 27: "In that crescent, . . ." Barry J. Beitzel, *The Moody Atlas of Bible Lands* (Chicago: Moody Press, 1985), 5.

p. 29: "He was a man . . ." Flavius Josephus, quoted in Michael E. Stone and Theodore A. Bergen, eds., *Biblical Figures Outside the Bible* (Harrisburg, Pa.: Trinity Press International, 1998), 160.

p. 29: "When our father Abraham . . ." Hayim Nahman Bialik and Yehosua Hana Ravnitzky, eds., *The Book of Legends: Sefer Ha-Aggadah. Legends from the Talmud and Midrash.* Trans. by William G. Braude (New York: Schocken Books, 1992), 31.

p. 31: "will issue a people . . ." Bialik and Ravnitzky, *The Book of Legends*, 31.

p. 31: "'Let us cut off . . ." Bialik and Ravnitzky, *The Book of Legends*, 31.

p. 31: "There is no might . . ." Bialik and Ravnitzky, *The Book of Legends*, 31.

p. 33: "If you were Lord . . ." Bialik and Ravnitzky, *The Book of Legends*, 32.

p. 33: "You are playing word games . . ." Bialik and Ravnitzky, *The Book of Legends*, 32.

CHAPTER THREE: ABRAM AND SARAI ON THE MOVE

p. 41: "[T]he Bible says . . ." Bruce Feiler, *Abraham: A Journey to the Heart of Three Faiths* (New York: William Morrow, 2002), 48–49.

p. 41:   "[W]hat did Abraham resemble? . . ." Bialik and Ravnitzky, *The Book of Legends*, 33.

p. 48:   "Such a slavery-based economy . . ." John Van Seters, *Abraham in History and Tradition* (New Haven and London: Yale University Press, 1975), 18.

CHAPTER FOUR: TRAVELS AND TRAVAILS

p. 52:   "When he was come to the place . . . Mary Loeffelholz, *Dickinson and the Boundaries of Feminist Theory* (Urbana: University of Illinois Press, 1991), 27.

p. 54:   "Another difficulty faced . . ." Victor H. Matthews, *Manners and Customs in the Bible* (Peabody, Mass.: Hendrickson Publishers, 1988), 10.

p. 56:   "'But Abraham is a . . ." Bialik and Ravnitzky, *The Book of Legends*, 34.

p. 57:   "there was not a path . . ." Bialik and Ravnitzky, *The Book of Legends*, 36.

p. 58:   "When a man would go . . ." Bialik and Ravnitzky, *The Book of Legends*, 36.

p. 59:   "The Bible suggests it was . . ." Karen Farrington, *Historical Atlas of the Holy Lands* (New York: Checkmark Books, 2003), 18–19.

CHAPTER FIVE: GOD'S COVENANT WITH ABRAHAM

p. 63:   "It has been suggested . . ." Beitzel, *The Moody Atlas of Bible Lands*, 46.

p. 71:   "*h* signifies God . . ." Gustav Dreifuss and Judith Riemer, *Abraham: The Man and the Symbol. A Jungian Interpretation of the Biblical Story* (Wilmette, Ill.: Chiron Publications, 1995), 49.

CHAPTER SIX: THE PROMISED CHILD

p. 73:   "Our father Abraham . . ." Bialik and Ravnitzky, *The Book of Legends*, 33.

p. 76:   "For years the tale . . ." Farrington, *Historical Atlas of the Holy Lands*, 19.

Chapter Seven: The Ultimate Test

p. 89: "Is it not . . . " Bialik and Ravnitzky, *The Book of Legends*, 39.

p. 89: "Abraham said to Sarah ..." Bialik and Ravnitzky, *The Book of Legends*, 40.

p. 90: "The binding of Abraham's favored ..." Feiler, *Abraham: A Journey to the Heart of Three Faiths*, 84.

p. 90: "Abraham is a true believer ..." Feiler, *Abraham: A Journey to the Heart of Three Faiths*, 104.

p. 92: "When Abraham entered after it ..." Bialik and Ravnitzky, *The Book of Legends*, 35.

p. 94: "All the damsels said . . ." Louis Ginzberg, *Legends of the Jews*, vol. 1 (Philadelphia: The Jewish Publication Society, 2003), 239–240.

Glossary

agrarian—relating to land or land use; rural, agricultural.

archaeology—the study of past civilizations or cultures by digging up or uncovering the remains of what people made or built, and then analyzing the role these artifacts played in people's lives.

artifact—a manmade object, and often one that is to be used for a specific purpose.

circumcision—to remove the foreskin of the male sexual organ.

coprolite—fossilized fecal remains of humans or animals.

covenant—an arrangement between two or more people in which they agree to do certain actions or accept certain obligations or responsibilities.

Dead Sea Scrolls—the Dead Sea Scrolls were discovered between 1947 and 1956 in eleven caves at Qumran near the Dead Sea. Among the scrolls are copies of parts of the Old Testament.

expulsion—the act of forcing out.

famine—an extreme scarcity of food over a wide geographical area.

genealogy—the different generations of ancestors that make up a person's "family tree."

geology—the scientific study of the origin, history, and structure of the earth.

heir—a person who will receive possessions and property from another person after their death.

idol—an image in wood, stone, or metal which represents a "god."

metaphor—an image or idea that combines two objects that seem dissimilar and shows how they are actually similar. When it is used as an adjective, it refers to a comparison that should not be taken literally.

monotheism—the belief in only one God ("mono" means "one" in Greek).

nomad—any wanderer, itinerant; a member of a group or tribe that moves about from place to place.

patriarch—an important father figure from whom families, tribes, or even races of people are descended. If the figure is a woman, she is called a matriarch.

polytheism—the belief in many gods ("poly" means "many" in Greek).

prefiguration—a person who comes earlier in time than someone else, and who represents that later figure and shares many of their same characteristics.

prophet—a person who communicates God's word or who speaks through divine inspiration. A woman is called a prophetess.

seismic—relating to earthquakes.

topography—the description of a geographic area which gives details about features such as hills, mountains, valleys, rivers, cities, and towns.

wean—to finish nursing one's mother's milk and change to a diet of solid foods.

Further Reading

FOR YOUNG READERS

Evslin, Bernard. *Signs and Wonders: Tales from the Old Testament*. New York: Four Winds Press, 1981.

Farrington, Karen. *Historical Atlas of the Holy Lands*. New York: Checkmark Books, 2003.

Gerstein, Mordicai. *The White Ram: A Story of Abraham and Isaac*. New York: Holiday House, 2006.

Millard, Alan. *Treasures from Bible Times*. Tring, Herts, UK: Lion Publishing, 1985.

Motyer, Stephen. *Who's Who in the Bible*. London: DK Publishing, 1998.

Segal, Lore, and Leonard Baskin. *The Book of Adam to Moses*. New York: Alfred A. Knopf, 1987.

Senker, Cath. *Everyday Life in the Bible Lands*. North Mankato, Minn.: Smart Apple Media, 2006.

van Loon, Hendrik Willem. *The Story of the Bible*. New York: Liveright, 1951.

FOR ADULTS

Chittister, Joan, OSB, Murshid Saadi Shakur Chishti, and Rabbi Arthur Waskow. *The Tent of Abraham: Stories of Hope and Peace for Jews, Christians, and Muslims*. Boston: Beacon Press, 2006.

Delaney, Carol. *Abraham on Trial: The Social Legacy of Biblical Myth*. Princeton, N.J.: Princeton University Press, 1998.

Dreifuss, Gustav, and Judith Riemer. *Abraham: The Man and the Symbol. A Jungian Interpretation of the Biblical Story*. Wilmette, Ill.: Chiron Publications, 1995.

Feiler, Bruce. *Abraham: A Journey to the Heart of Three Faiths*. New York: William Morrow, 2002.

Kaltner, John. *Ishmael Instructs Isaac: An Introduction to the Qur'an for Bible Readers*. Collegeville, Minn.: The Liturgical Press, 1999.

King, Philip J., and Lawrence E. Stager. *Life in Biblical Israel*. Louisville and London: Westminster John Knox Press, 2001.

Rogerson, John. *Atlas of the Bible*. New York: Facts on File Publications, 1985.

Van Seters, John. *Abraham in History and Tradition*. New Haven and London: Yale University Press, 1975.

Internet Resources

Bible Tutor
www.demo.lutherproductions.com/bibletutor

> An excellent general introduction to both the Old and New Testaments, aimed at a young audience, but also useful for adults. It is divided into categories such as Books, People, Dates, and Places; within each category are short but very clear descriptions and links to other pages in the Tutor, photos, and biblical passages. The Basic Level has free access online, but the Advanced Level must be purchased from Luther Productions (Luther Seminary, St. Paul, Minnesota).

Biblical Art on the World Wide Web
www.biblical-art.com

> A marvelous Web site with art from ancient to modern times. Artwork can be searched by subject, text, artist, and word. Click on [Image] to enlarge the thumbnail photos. Note: be sure to include the hyphen when you type in the address.

The British Museum
www.britishmuseum.org

> At this site's home page, search for Ancient Israel, which will bring up a gallery of photos of artifacts and their histories. A particularly nice feature here are the links you can

use to visit related themes, galleries, cultures, and tours. There is also an excellent online tour of the Middle East.

Canaan and Ancient Israel
www.museum.upenn.edu/Canaan/index.html

A wonderful online exhibit, operated by the University of Pennsylvania Museum of Archaeology and Anthropology, about the land of Canaan, with pages detailing the land, economy, religion, and daily life. Each section has a glossary, bibliography, activities designed for children ages eight to twelve, and links to other sites of interest. The activities feature projects that children can do at home, as well as themes and questions to help them think about what connections they can make between this exhibit and their own lives. If you go to the Museum's home page—www.museum.upenn.edu—there are links to online exhibits, including a spectacular one titled "Treasures from the Royal Tombs of Ur."

The Hebrews: A Learning Module
www.wsu.edu/~dee/HEBREWS/HEBREWS.HTM

This site, designed primarily for college freshmen, features a very detailed overview of the history of the Hebrews from the Patriarchal Age to the Diaspora. It is mostly text, with a huge amount of information, but there are also links to related subjects such as Egypt. It is part of World Civilizations: An Internet Classroom and Anthology, a project of Washington State University.

Heritage: Civilization and the Jews
www.pbs.org/wnet/heritage

This site offers a detailed history of the Jews from their beginnings to modern times. Episode 1, "Beginnings," features interactive presentations and atlases, timelines, and video resources. There is also a page with lesson plans for middle and high school teachers, with abundant resources. This series is also available for purchase as a DVD or video.

The Israel Museum
www.english.imjnet.org.il

At this site's home page, go to Galleries and then to Archaeology Wing to view artifacts from the Museum's collections. Introductory texts feature a general introduction to time periods from prehistory to the Islamic period, and include examples of artifacts with explanatory texts and photos that can be enlarged to really show interesting details of each piece. Another interesting feature of this museum which needs to be reached through a separate address is: "Imagine: The Image Search Engine of the Israel Museum."

The Jewish Museum
www.thejewishmuseum.org

At this site, go first to Collection and Exhibitions, then to Collections Overview for a wide selection of antiquities from the Museum's permanent collection. Each page gives a history of the artifact, and then allows you to view it with zoom, pan, and 3D features. It's as close as you'll come to actually touching the artifact. There is also a selection of online exhibits.

Jewish Virtual Library
www.jewishvirtuallibrary.org

This site offers a comprehensive look at Jewish history from ancient to modern times, and has a number of pages dedicated to archaeology and ancient history. The archaeology page has a huge section on excavation sites, many of which include photos. The text is very readable and offers a wealth of details.

Introduction to the Hebrew Bible
www.hope.edu/bandstra/RTOT/RTOT.HTM

Designed for older students, this website features a survey of the Old Testament, with summaries of stories and links to the relevant biblical passages. There is a lot of background information which includes some photos. Each Study Guide section includes a chapter summary, key terms, and interesting concept questions. This is also available as a hardcover book and CD from Wadsworth/Thomson Learning (some features are available only on the CD).

Index

Aaron, 30
Abel and Cain, 14
Abimelech (king of Gerar), 6, 22, 82–84
Abraham
    and Abimelech, 82–84
    archaeological evidence of, 15–17, 19
    banishes Hagar, 79–82
    and Canaan, 35, 38–49, 55–59, 61–65
    children of, 68–71, 77–82, 95–96
    and the covenant, 15, 61, 65–67, 70–71
    death and burial, 96
    early life, 25–26, 28–29, 31–35
    faith of, 22, 40, 66–67, 88, 90, 97–98
    in Haran, 36–38
    importance of, 13–15, 40–41, 98–99, 101
    marries Keturah, 95–96
    lies about Sarah, 22, 50–54, 82–83
    lifespan of, 23
    monotheism of, 11, 13, 25, 29, 31–34, 64–65
    name change of, from Abram, 26, 70–71
    sacrifice of son Isaac, 10–12, 85–87, 89–90
    and Sodom and Gomorrah, 72–77
    travels to Egypt, 49–55
    travels to Mecca with Ishmael, 80–81
    and war in Canaan, 61–65
    wealth of, 6, 7, 19–22, 49, 52, 55, 56, 83, 97–99
    See also Canaan; Isaac (Abraham's son); Ishmael (Abraham's son)
Abraham: A Journey to the Heart of Three Faiths (Feiler), 90
Abraham: The Man and the Symbol (Dreifuss and Riemer), 71
Abraham in History and Tradition (Van Seters), 48
Abram. *See* Abraham
Adam, 14, 23–24, 81, 92
Ai, *46*, 47, 48
Albright, William F., 20
Ammonites, 88
Amos, 9
Aner, 63, 65
Angel of God, 73–74
archaeological excavations, 16–17, 19, 26, 48, 49, 60, 76, 99
Assyria, 20, 27
Azar (Abraham's father, in Islam), 34–35

Babylon, 20, *25*
Babylonia, 27
barter, 20
    See also wealth
Beersheba, 82, 84, 87
Beitzel, Barry J., 27, 63
Beltrano, Agostino, *86*

Numbers in ***bold italics*** refer to captions.

Bera (King of Sodom), 64–65
Bethel, 47, 48
Bethuel, 95
Bible, 7–9, 13–15, 16, 19–20, 30, 45, 74, 79, 99
  Canaan's location, 58–59
  and Sodom and Gomorrah, 73
  See also Genesis passages
Bible of Borgo d'Este, *53*
Bible of Jean de Sy, *57*
binding, 88–90
  See also sacrifices
bitumen, 62, 63

Cain and Abel, 14
Canaan, 6, 29, 35, *37*, 67, 70
  Abraham's journey to, 38–49
  Abraham's return to, 55–59
  borders of, 41–43, 58–60
  placement of, on trade routes, 20–21
  warfare in, 43, 61–65
  See also Abraham
caravans, 20, 28, 42
  See also trade
Carchemish, 36
cattle, 55
Chaldeans, 26
Chedorlaomer (King), 61–63
Christianity, *12*, 13, 14, 41, 80, 90, 98–99, 101
  See also Islam; Judaism
circumcision, 70
Cortona, Pietro da, *69*
covenant, 15, 61, 65–67, 70–71
  See also Abraham
cuneiform, *28*
currency, 6, 20, 83
  See also wealth

Dan, 63
Dead Sea, 76
Dead Sea Scrolls, 30
Deuteronomy, 8, 79
  See also Bible
Documentary Hypothesis, 14–15
  See also Bible
Doré, Gustave, *40*, *76*, *92*
Dreifuss, Gustav, 71

Ebal (Mount), 46

Egypt, 17, 20, 36, 42–43, 49–55, 56, 68, 80, 82
Elam, 61–63
Eliezer, *66*, 67, 93–95
Ephron, 90
Epistle to the Hebrews, 30
  See also Bible
Eshcol, 63, 65
Euphrates River, 26, 27
Eve, 14, 23–24
  See also Adam
Exodus, 79
  See also Bible

famine, 49–50, 88
Farrington, Karen, 59, 76
Feiler, Bruce, 41, 90
Fertile Crescent, 27, 36
  See also Mesopotamia
firstborn sons, 78, 79
flood, 24, *81*

Gabriel (Angel), *12*, 16
Garden of Eden, 23–24, 26
Gaza Strip, 41
Genesis passages, 7–8, 13, 14–15, 16, 19, 35, 48, 65, 93
  Abimelech, 83, 84
  Abraham's banishment of Hagar, 79–80
  Abraham's death, 96
  Abraham's journey to Haran, 37–38
  Abraham's name change, 70
  Abraham's wealth, 6, 7, 52, 56, 98
  Adam and Eve, 23–24
  Canaan, 58–59
  circumcision, 70
  and famine, 49
  God speaks to Abraham about Canaan, 38, 46
  God's covenant with Abraham, 61, 65–67, 70–71
  Isaac, 71, 77, 85–87
  Ishmael, *69*, 82
  Lot's land choosing, 56–58
  Melchizedek, 30, 64
  Noah, 24–25
  Rebekah, 95
  Sarah, 50–51, 53
  Sodom and Gomorrah, 74–77

See also Abraham; Bible
Gerar, 82–83
Gerizim (Mount), 46
Gilgamesh, 31
Golden Haggadah, *21*
Gomorrah, 57, 62–63, 72–77
Great Trunk Road, 36

Hagar, 14, 67–69, 70, 74, 77–80, 82, 96
  See also Abraham; Ishmael (Abraham's son)
Haran (Abraham's brother), 34, 36
Haran (city), 36–38, 93
Harran, Turkey, 36
Hebron, 61, 84, 90, 96
Historical Atlas of the Holy Lands (Farrington), 59, 76
Hittites, *37*
hospitality, 72–73, 82

insects, 45–46
Iraq, 26, 27
Isaac (Abraham's son), 8, 14, 71, 77–78, 80, 96
  Abraham's attempted sacrifice of, 10–12, 85–87, 89–90
  marries Rebekah, 93–95
  See also Abraham; Sarah (Abraham's wife)
Isaiah, 9
Ishbak (Abraham's son), 95
Ishmael (Abraham's son), 14, 68–70, 71, 77–82, 87–89, *91*, 96
  See also Abraham; Hagar; Islam
Ishmaelites, 16–17, 82
Islam, *12*, 13–14, 41, 80–81, 90, *91*, 98, 101
  and Hagar, 68
  and the Qur'an, 16, 34–35, 87–88
  See also Christianity; Judaism
Israel, 8–9, 16, 41
Israelites, 16–17

Jacob, 8, 14, 74
Jesus Christ, 7, 9, 30
Job, 8
Jokshan (Abraham's son), 95
Jordan, 41, 57, *58*
Joseph, 8, 14

Josephus, Flavius, 29
Judaism, *12*, 13–14, *21*, 41, 68, 80, 90, 98, 101
  See also Christianity; Islam

Ka'aba, 81
  See also Islam
Keturah (Abraham's wife), 95–96

Lebanon, 41, 45
legends and folktales, Jewish. *See* tradition, Jewish
Letter to the Romans, 14–15, 22
Leviticus, 79
  See also Bible
Lievens the Elder, Jan, *86*
Lot (Abraham's nephew), 6, 36, 56–58, 61, 63, 74–75, 77

Machpelah (cave), 90, 92–93, 96
Mamre, 63, 65
Mandela, Nelson, 55
Manners and Customs in the Bible (Matthews), 54
maps, 18, 27
Maqam Ibrahim (Station of Abraham), 81
Matthews, Victor, 54
Mecca, 80–81
Medan (Abraham's son), 95
Melchizedek, 28, 30, 63–64, *65*
Mesopotamia, 17, 26, 27, 28, 29, 31, 42–43, 61–63, 64
Midian (Abraham's son), 95
Midrash (Jewish), 29, 31, 32, *94*
  See also tradition, Jewish
Moabites, 88
monotheism, 6, 11, 13, 25, 29, 31–34, 64–65
The Moody Atlas of Bible Lands (Beitzel), 27, 63
Moses, 13, 14, 74, 79
Muhammad, 16, 82
  See also Islam

Nablus, Israel, 46
Nahor (Abraham's brother), 95
Nanna (moon-god), 28
Negev, 47, 80, 87
New Testament, 13

See also Bible
Nimrod (King), 6, *21*, 25, 29, 31, 33–34
Noah, 8, 14, 24–25, *81*
nomads, 20, 40, *42*, 45, 47–48

Old Testament. *See* Bible

Paul (Apostle), 14–15, 22, 30
Persian Gulf, 26, 28
Pharaoh, 22, 52–54, 55
   See also Egypt
Phoenicia, 20
polytheism, 11, 13, 25, 28, 64–65
Promised Land, 35, 46, 67, 70
   See also Canaan
Proverbs, 8
   See also Bible

Qur'an, 15, 16, 34–35, 87–88
   See also Islam

Rebekah, 93–95
   See also Isaac (Abraham's son)
religion, *12*, 13–14
   and wealth, 7–9
   See also Christianity; Islam; Judaism
Rembrandt, 10, 73
Riemer, Judith, 71
Rubens, Peter Paul, *65*

sacrifices, 10–12, 47, 67, 85–90, *91*
Salem (Jerusalem), 30, 63–64, *65*
Sarah (Abraham's wife), 13–14, 21–22, 81–83, 89
   archaeological evidence of, 15–17, 19
   in Canaan, 43–49
   death and burial of, 90, 92–93
   and Hagar, 67–68, 77–79
   in Haran, 36–38
   hospitality of, 72–73
   is given to Pharaoh, 50–53
   and Isaac, 71–73, 77–78
   name change of, from Sarai, 70–71
   returns to Canaan, 55
   travels to Egypt, 49–55
   wealth of, 6, 21–22
   See also Abraham; Isaac (Abraham's son)

Sarai. *See* Sarah (Abraham's wife)
Satan, 89
Sermon on the Mount, 7
Shechem, 46–47
shekels, 6, 83, 98
   See also currency
Shuah (Abraham's son), 95
silver, 20
slavery, 38, 48
Sodom, 57, *58*, 62–63, 64–65, 72–77
Solomon, 8
Sumer, 27
Syria, 20, 41
Syrian Desert, 42

Tarsus, 36
Terah (Abraham's father), 29, 31–33, 36–37
   death of, 38
Tigris River, 27
tithing, 64
Tomb of the Patriarchs, 90, 92, 96, *100*
Torah, 15, 29, 38, 79
   See also Bible
Tower of Babel, 14, *25*
trade, 20–21, 28, 37, 42–43, 63
tradition, Jewish, 15–16, 28–29, 56, 57, 68, 77, 81–82, 89
Turkey, 26, 36, *37*, 41

Ur of the Chaldees, 26, 28, 29, *32*, 35, 36, 59

Valley of Siddim, 61–62
Van Seters, John, 48

wealth, 20
   of Abraham, 6, 7, 19–21, 49, 52, 55, 56, 83, 97–99
   and religion, 6, 7–9
West Bank, 41
Woolley, Charles (Sir), 26

Yahweh, 16

Ziggurat of Ur, *26*, *32*
Zimran (Abraham's son), 95
Zwelithini, Goodwill, 55

Illustration Credits

2: Bildarchiv Preussischer Kulturbesitz/Art Resource, NY
10: Scala/Art Resource, NY
12: Erich Lessing/Art Resource, NY
13: Tor Eigeland/Saudi Aramco World/PADIA
17: © 2008 Jupiterimages Corporation
18: © OTTN Publishing
21: HIP/Art Resource, NY
24: © 2008 Jupiterimages Corporation
25: © 2008 Jupiterimages Corporation
26: Tor Eigeland/Saudi Aramco World/PADIA
27: © Norman Einstein
28: Used under license from Shutterstock, Inc.
30: Used under license from Shutterstock, Inc.
32: Tor Eigeland/Saudi Aramco World/PADIA
33: Erich Lessing/Art Resource, NY
37: © 2008 Jupiterimages Corporation
39: Ms 139/1363 fol.33r *The Calling of Abraham and Lot Leaving Sodom*, from 'Le Miroir de l'Humaine Salvation' (vellum) by Flemish School, (15th century). Musee Conde, Chantilly, France/ Lauros / Giraudon/ The Bridgeman Art Library.
40: Courtesy Creationism.org
42: Tor Eigeland/Saudi Aramco World/PADIA
44: *The Journey of Abraham and Lot*, 1356–67 (fresco) by also Manfredi de Battilori Bartolo di Fredi (1330–1410). Collegiata, San Gimignano, Italy/ Alinari/ The Bridgeman Art Library
46: Erich Lessing/Art Resource, NY
47: Erich Lessing/Art Resource, NY
51: Used under license from Shutterstock, Inc.
53: Scala/Art Resource, NY
54: Used under license from Shutterstock, Inc.
57: *Abraham and Sarah leave Ur of the Chaldees for Canaan*, from 'The Bible of Jean de Sy', c.1355 (vellum) by French School (14th century). Bibliotheque Nationale, Paris, France/ Giraudon/ The Bridgeman Art Library.
58: © 2008 Jupiterimages Corporation
62: Used under license from Shutterstock, Inc.
65: Erich Lessing/Art Resource, NY
66: Used under license from Shutterstock, Inc.
69: Erich Lessing/Art Resource, NY
73: *Abraham Receives the Three Angels* by Rembrandt Harmensz. van Rijn (1606–69). Aurora Trust/ The Bridgeman Art Library.
75: © 2008 Jupiterimages Corporation
76: Courtesy Creationism.org
78: *The Expulsion of Hagar and Ishmael*, c.1644 (oil on canvas) by Jan Victors (1620–76). Private Collection/ Johnny Van Haeften Ltd., London/ The Bridgeman Art Library.
81: Used under license from Shutterstock, Inc.
86: Alinari/Art Resource, NY
87: Erich Lessing/Art Resource, NY
89: © 2008 Jupiterimages Corporation
91: © 2008 Jupiterimages Corporation
92: Courtesy Creationism.org
94: Erich Lessing/Art Resource, NY
99: Used under license from Shutterstock, Inc.
100: Used under license from Shutterstock, Inc.
Cover: © 2008 Jupiterimages Corporation

DENISE-RENÉE BARBERET has a doctorate in medieval Spanish literature, and has taught at colleges and universities in Massachusetts for the last twenty years. Her scholarly research has concentrated on depictions of women in medieval texts. She is currently an editor and freelance writer, and prefers to write about the ordinary and the unexpected, which are sometimes not as far apart as one might think. She is also a licensed EMT.